Gleanings from
RUTH

Gleanings from RUTH

Dr. Janet Walsh

Sword of the Lord

Post Office Box 1099 • Murfreesboro, Tennessee 37133
(800) 247-9673 • (615) 893-6700 • FAX (615) 278-1309
swordofthelord.com

Contents

Trusting Brings Blessing

"Trust in the LORD, and do good; so shalt thou dwell in the land, and verily thou shalt be fed."—
Ps. 37:3.

The Book of Ruth is a little book tucked among the books of history in the Bible. It is a nice story about a girl from "the wrong side of the tracks" who left everything she knew after her husband's death to go to her mother-in-law's homeland, where she found true love and everyone lived happily ever after. We can assuredly say, however, that God gave us this story for a reason much greater than mere entertainment.

There is much truth to be learned from this little book. We can learn some history, some culture and some great spiritual lessons in the four short chapters of Ruth. This book brings the everyday life of its characters into vivid reality.

In the Old Testament books of history, we read about kingdoms and wars and prophets' ministries. What was going on while those things were taking place? Ordinary people got up each morning, made breakfast, taught their children, and lived through everyday trials and triumphs. We may overlook those ordinary people, but they were there. We must never forget that the people living in that time were real people. They had feelings, concerns, laughter, and sorrow.

I. "In the Days When the Judges Ruled"

"Now it came to pass in the days when the judges ruled, that there was a famine in the land. And a certain man of Beth-lehem-Judah went to sojourn in the country of Moab, he, and his wife, and his two sons.

"And the name of the man was Elimelech, and the name of his wife Naomi, and the name of his two sons Mahlon and Chilion, Ephrathites of Beth-lehem-Judah. And they came into the country of Moab, and continued there.

"And Elimelech Naomi's husband died; and she was left, and her two sons.

"And they took them wives of the women of Moab; the name of the one was Orpah, and the name of the other Ruth: and they dwelled there about ten years.

"And Mahlon and Chilion died also both of them; and the woman was left of her two sons and her husband."—Ruth 1:1–5.

Notice that verse 1 says that the judges ruled. It does not say that God ruled. The people of Israel were originally supposed to be a theocracy—that is, God was in charge, and they were to obey Him. God was to rule in the lives and affairs of the people.

Instead, during this period of Israel's history, the judges ruled. The people did not want to follow God's commandments. "Every man did that which was right in his own eyes" (Judg. 17:6; 21:25). When every man does that which is right in his own eyes, there may be some who will follow God, His Word and His commandments; but generally people will go farther and farther from God.

If you are going to stay on track with God, you must do that on purpose. It is easy for people to drift away from God.

> *"Wide is the gate, and broad is the way, that leadeth to destruction, and many there be which go in thereat:*
>
> *"Because strait is the gate, and narrow is the way, which leadeth unto life, and few there be that find it."*— Matt. 7:13,14.

In the Book of Judges, we see a nasty cycle repeated over and over.

1. The people of Israel disobeyed God.
2. God allowed enemies to oppress them.
3. The people cried out to God.
4. God sent a judge to deliver His people from the enemy.
5. There was a time of peace.

This was followed by a repeat of these five steps.

The story of Ruth takes place sometime during the time of the judges. There is quite a difference among Bible scholars' estimates of when it took place. Some put it during the time of Deborah in Judges 4 and 5; some say that it was during the time of Gideon in Judges 6 and 7; while others say that it took place during the time of Samson in Judges 13–16.

We cannot know for sure the exact place in the time of the judges the story of Ruth happened, but it was apparently during one of the times of peace and rest. There is nothing to indicate that the people feared for their safety in the face of enemies. There were difficulties in the lives of the characters in the Book of Ruth, but they were not caused by fear of enemy attack or oppression.

During the time of the Book of Judges, the people drifted farther and farther from God. When Joshua was alive, he led the people in obeying God's commands; but after Joshua's death and after all those who knew Joshua were dead, the people turned away from God and went into the time of the judges. "And Israel served the LORD all the days of Joshua, and all the days of the elders that overlived Joshua, and which had known all the works of the LORD, that he had done for Israel" (Josh. 24:31).

As long as Joshua was alive, the people did well.

> "And Joshua the son of Nun, the servant of the LORD, died, being an hundred and ten years old.
>
> "And they buried him in the border of his inheritance in Timnath-heres, in the mount of Ephraim, on the north side of the hill Gaash.
>
> "And also all that generation were gathered unto their fathers: and there arose another generation after them, which knew not the LORD, nor yet the works which he had done for Israel.
>
> "And the children of Israel did evil in the sight of the LORD, and served Baalim:
>
> "And they forsook the LORD God of their fathers, which brought them out of the land of Egypt, and followed other gods, of the gods of the people that were round about them, and bowed themselves unto them, and provoked the LORD to anger."—Judg. 2:8–12.

God gave the land of Canaan to the people of Israel and told them to drive out all the inhabitants. They were to claim the land for themselves and not live among the heathen people who had lived there before them.

However, we see in the Book of Judges that they did not accomplish that task.

"And the LORD was with Judah; and he drave out the inhabitants of the mountain; but could not drive out the inhabitants of the valley, because they had chariots of iron."

"And the children of Benjamin did not drive out the Jebusites that inhabited Jerusalem; but the Jebusites dwell with the children of Benjamin in Jerusalem unto this day."

"Neither did Manasseh drive out the inhabitants of Beth-shean and her towns, nor Taanach and her towns, nor the inhabitants of Dor and her towns, nor the inhabitants of Ibleam and her towns, nor the inhabitants of Megiddo and her towns: but the Canaanites would dwell in that land.

"And it came to pass, when Israel was strong, that they put the Canaanites to tribute, and did not utterly drive them out.

"Neither did Ephraim drive out the Canaanites that dwelt in Gezer; but the Canaanites dwelt in Gezer among them.

"Neither did Zebulun drive out the inhabitants of Kitron, nor the inhabitants of Nahalol; but the Canaanites dwelt among them, and became tributaries.

"Neither did Asher drive out the inhabitants of Accho, nor the inhabitants of Zidon, nor of Ahlab, nor of Achzib, nor of Helbah, nor of Aphik, nor of Rehob:

"But the Asherites dwelt among the Canaanites, the inhabitants of the land: for they did not drive them out.

"Neither did Naphtali drive out the inhabitants of Beth-shemeth, nor the inhabitants of Beth-anath;

> *but he dwelt among the Canaanites, the inhabitants of the land: nevertheless the inhabitants of Beth-shemeth and of Beth-anath became tributaries unto them.*
>
> *"And the Amorites forced the children of Dan into the mountain: for they would not suffer them to come down to the valley."*—1:19, 21, 27-34.

God gave His people the land of Canaan and told them to drive out its inhabitants, but they did not do that. Instead, they lived among them, and that was where they got themselves into trouble. God wanted His people to drive out the heathen so that His own would remain in fellowship with Him, worshiping and obeying Him. He knew what would happen if they got too close to the heathen people. We also know that we must always choose our friends wisely.

As always, God was right. The Book of Judges reveals that the Israelites lived next to heathen, became their friends, and allowed their children to marry the children of the heathen; consequently, they learned heathen ways. They learned about worship of the false gods of the people in that land. God had warned them against that very thing.

The Book of Judges also shows that there were nearly always some people who determined to keep their hearts right before God. Over and over again when the people of Israel cried out to God because of the oppression of their enemies, God raised up a judge who would obey Him, and the people were delivered.

It was not only the judges who kept their hearts right with God. There were many ordinary people in the land that we read nothing about in the pages of Scripture. They escape our notice because the Bible does not record their daily, routine lives. The people in the Book of Ruth are just such people.

II. To Moab to Escape the Famine

Naomi and Elimelech decided to move to the land of Moab. They had been living in Bethlehem. It is interesting to notice that the name *Bethlehem* means "the house of bread and praise," yet there was a famine in that place.

You will also notice that Bethlehem was in the land of Canaan, which was the land that God had promised to the people of Israel. He had told them that it was a land flowing with milk and honey. When God called to Moses out of the burning bush, He told him about the land that He would give His people. "And I am come down to deliver them out of the hand of the Egyptians, and to bring them up out of that land unto a good land and a large, unto a land flowing with milk and honey" (Exod. 3:8).

When the spies returned from Canaan, they brought back the amazing fruit from the land to show to the people. "And they came unto the brook of Eshcol, and cut down from thence a branch with one cluster of grapes, and they bare it between two upon a staff; and they brought of the pomegranates, and of the figs" (Num. 13:23). "And they told him [Moses], and said, We came unto the land whither thou sentest us, and surely it floweth with milk and honey; and this is the fruit of it" (vs. 27).

Everything grew beautifully. It was a wonderful land in which to live, yet there was a famine there during the lifetime of Ruth. God had told the people that the plenty in the land was a blessing from Him if they obeyed Him.

"And it shall come to pass, if thou shalt hearken diligently unto the voice of the LORD thy God, to observe and to do all his commandments which I command thee this day, that the LORD thy God will set thee on high above all nations of the earth:

"And all these blessings shall come on thee, and overtake thee, if thou shalt hearken unto the voice of the LORD thy God."

"Blessed shall be the fruit of thy body, and the fruit of thy ground, and the fruit of thy cattle, and the increase of thy kine, and the flocks of thy sheep.

"Blessed shall be thy basket and thy store."

"The LORD shall command the blessing upon thee in thy storehouses, and in all that thou settest thine hand unto; and he shall bless thee in the land which the LORD thy God giveth thee.

"The LORD shall establish thee an holy people unto himself, as he hath sworn unto thee, if thou shalt keep the commandments of the LORD thy God, and walk in his ways."

"And the LORD shall make thee plenteous in goods, in the fruit of thy body, and in the fruit of thy cattle, and in the fruit of thy ground, in the land which the LORD sware unto thy fathers to give thee."—Deut. 28:1, 2, 4, 5, 8, 9, 11.

The land would grow plenty of food for them, their flocks would produce many offspring, and they themselves would be fruitful in having many children. These were wonderful blessings promised to the people of Israel, but they were all conditional. The Israelites would receive those blessings only if they continued to obey God.

On the other hand, if they chose to turn away from

God, the judgments would be just as severe as the blessings were bountiful.

> "But it shall come to pass, if thou wilt not hearken unto the voice of the LORD thy God, to observe to do all his commandments and his statutes which I command thee this day; that all these curses shall come upon thee, and overtake thee:
>
> "Cursed shalt thou be in the city, and cursed shalt thou be in the field.
>
> "Cursed shall be thy basket and thy store.
>
> "Cursed shall be the fruit of thy body, and the fruit of thy land, the increase of thy kine, and the flocks of thy sheep.
>
> "Cursed shalt thou be when thou comest in, and cursed shalt thou be when thou goest out."—Vss. 15–19.

The famine was a judgment against Israel because they had repeatedly disobeyed the Lord. In the land of Moab, however, there was bread.

We may ask, then, why there was food in the land of Moab when they had never been a people of God. They were not obeying Him either, so why were they not receiving the same chastisement that was coming from God to the people of Israel?

When asking that question, we must remember that chastisement from God comes to His children. The people of Moab were not His people. The judgment from God was upon Israel to get their attention.

We know that we do not chasten other people's children as we chasten our own. When we see in our own children a behavior that is not right, we chasten them because they are a blessing to us from God and we have a responsibility before God to train them to do right.

That responsibility for other children falls to their parents. God was chastening His own.

The people of Israel could have looked at the people of Moab and wondered why they were being blessed with food. They could have wondered, *We are the people of God, and we have no food. They are disobeying God as well, but they have food.* We must not look at what appears to be blessings on others if they are not obeying God.

> *"Fret not thyself because of evildoers, neither be thou envious against the workers of iniquity.*
>
> *"For they shall soon be cut down like the grass, and wither as the green herb."*—Ps. 37:1, 2.

Conclusion

The fact is that the people of Moab were getting their rewards in this life only. God has something better for His people. He works in our lives, sometimes making life miserable for us, because He wants us to keep our focus on Him. The chastisement that God sends is for our good. He sends it so that we will get our hearts and minds back on Him.

"Trust in the LORD, and do good; so shalt thou dwell in the land, and verily thou shalt be fed" (vs. 3). We must trust God. We may not always understand what He is doing; but if we keep our eyes on Him, we will keep our focus on the right things. When God chastens, even if we do not understand what He is trying to teach us, we must get our eyes, heart and mind on Him. If, however, we try to escape the chastisement which God sends to get our attention, we will not learn the lesson He is trying to teach us, and the chastisement will last longer.

Naomi lived in Moab for ten years. During that time, Elimelech died, and so did their two sons. When Naomi returned to Bethlehem, the famine had been over for a while: they were harvesting grain.

Did the chastisement for Naomi last longer than it needed to last? Would she have had a shorter time of difficulty if she had stayed in the land of Israel? Would her husband and sons have survived if they had stayed in Israel? Of course we cannot know the answers to these questions, but we know this: God blesses His children who obey and serve Him, and He chastens those who do not.

Starting with the opening verse of the Book of Ruth, we can see that we must simply trust God. In all areas of our lives, we must settle in our hearts that God is in control. If we obey Him, He will bless. If we disobey, He will do something to get our attention. Trust God.

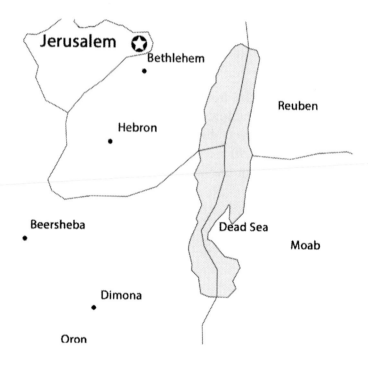

Who Was Moab?

"Blessed is the man that feareth the LORD, that delighteth greatly in his commandments.

"The wicked shall see it, and be grieved."—Ps. 112:1, 10.

We have seen that the story of Ruth took place during the time of the judges, when the people were not trusting and obeying God but were doing whatever they thought was right. They did what they wanted to do. We also saw that Naomi and Elimelech left Bethlehem in the land of Israel, which God had promised to them, in order to escape the famine in that land. When they left Israel, they went to Moab.

I have been curious about why they chose to go to Moab particularly, and we will not be able to answer that question because the Bible does not tell us. The fact is that they went to Moab thinking it would better their situation. There is a lesson in that for us.

In order to get to Moab, they had to cross the Jordan River. In doing so, they were in the land of Reuben which was still a part of the land of Israel but was adjacent to Moab. They could have stayed in the land of Israel if they had stayed in Reuben, but they passed through Reuben and went on to Moab.

I. Who Was Moab?

Abram had a nephew named Lot. "And Terah took Abram his son, and Lot the son of Haran his son's son" (Gen. 11:31).

After Abram's father died (vs. 32), Lot stayed with Abram. "And Abram took Sarai his wife, and Lot his brother's son, and all their substance that they had gathered, and the souls that they had gotten in Haran; and they went forth to go into the land of Canaan" (12:5).

Abram was very rich. "And Abram was very rich in cattle, in silver, and in gold" (13:2). Lot was also very rich. "And Lot also, which went with Abram, had flocks, and herds, and tents" (vs. 5).

Abram and Lot together had so much wealth that the land could not support them both. "And the land was not able to bear them, that they might dwell together: for their substance was great, so that they could not dwell together" (vs. 6).

The servants of the two men were fighting among themselves over water and pasture. Abram, as much as he loved Lot, suggested that they should go their separate ways so that there would be enough for all their flocks and servants.

> "And Abram said unto Lot, Let there be no strife, I pray thee, between me and thee, and between my herdmen and thy herdmen; for we be brethren.
>
> "Is not the whole land before thee? separate thyself, I pray thee, from me: if thou wilt take the left hand, then I will go to the right; or if thou depart to the right hand, then I will go to the left." —Vss. 8, 9.

Lot should have allowed Abram to have the first

choice of land out of respect for Abram as his elder and as the one who had taken care of him since his father had died. Lot did not do that; instead, he made the first choice. I think that in itself says something about his character. Then he chose for himself what he thought was the better land.

Abram's offering Lot first choice and being happy with what was left for himself says something positive about his character. Why was he willing to do that? Because he trusted God. God saw Abram's heart, and He would bless him because of it.

What did Lot choose? How did he make his choice?

> *"And Lot lifted up his eyes, and beheld all the plain of Jordan, that it was well watered every where, before the LORD destroyed Sodom and Gomorrah, even as the garden of the LORD, like the land of Egypt, as thou comest unto Zoar.*
>
> *"Then Lot chose him all the plain of Jordan; and Lot journeyed east: and they separated themselves the one from the other.*
>
> *"Abram dwelled in the land of Canaan, and Lot dwelled in the cities of the plain, and pitched his tent toward Sodom.*
>
> *"But the men of Sodom were wicked and sinners before the LORD exceedingly."*—Vss. 10–13.

On what did Lot base his decision? Verse 10 tells us that he looked for well-watered land where there would be plenty for his flocks. He pitched his tent near Sodom. He wanted a place where he could continue to grow in wealth. This seems logical, but verse 13 warns about the wickedness of the people in Sodom. Did Lot not notice this, or did he think it would not matter? Was it really that bad? After all, Lot was not in *among* the people of the city; he only had his tent *near* Sodom.

We can imagine what happened. His wife went into the city to shop. His daughters went into the city to shop and to socialize. They saw the fashionable young ladies there. They met the young men. They began to enjoy the excitement, the lights and the glamour of the city. They wanted to be more involved in it.

Genesis 14 records the account of a battle during which Lot and his family were captured and carried away.

> *"And they took all the goods of Sodom and Gomorrah, and all their victuals, and went their way.*
>
> *"And they took Lot, Abram's brother's son, who dwelt in Sodom, and his goods, and departed."* — Vss. 11,12.

By this time Lot was living in Sodom. It got him into trouble too. Abram came to his rescue. It must have made Abram very sad to know that Lot had gotten mixed up with those people, but he helped his nephew. "And when Abram heard that his brother was taken captive, he armed his trained servants, born in his own house, three hundred and eighteen, and pursued them unto Dan" (vs. 14). "And he brought back all the goods, and also brought again his brother Lot, and his goods, and the women also, and the people" (vs. 16).

Lot was not living *near* Sodom anymore. He was not living *near* the wickedness; he was living *in* it.

Genesis 18 says three men came to see Abraham with a message from God. They told him that God was going to destroy Sodom because of the exceeding nature of the sin. God knew that Lot lived there, and He knew that Abraham would want to know that He was going to destroy the city.

Abraham asked God if He would really destroy the righteous right along with the wicked. What if there were 50 righteous people there? God said He would not destroy the city if there were 50 righteous people there. What if there were only 45, or 40, or 30, or 20, or even only 10 righteous people there? Would He destroy the entire city if there were at least 10 righteous people there? God said He would not destroy the city if there were at least 10 righteous in it.

Surely, Abraham thought, *Lot has influenced some others for the Lord.* Surely the testimony of his nephew could save the city—or so he thought.

When the two angels went to Sodom, they found Lot at the gate. "And there came two angels to Sodom at even; and Lot sat in the gate of Sodom: and Lot seeing them rose up to meet them; and he bowed himself with his face toward the ground" (19:1).

In those days, the gate of the city was where the official business took place. There was probably a gate there, as we think of a gate, but it was also a meeting place for the officials of the city. It was where business transactions took place—the "courthouse." That was where the angels found Lot.

Lot did not live *near* Sodom anymore. Not only did he live *in* Sodom, but he had also become one of the city officials there. He was sitting at the gate. He was truly one *of* them!

The angels warned Lot that the city would be destroyed. He tried to warn his sons-in-law, but they did not believe him! They laughed at him! He had a wife and two daughters still living at home. In the morning, the angels tried to get him and his family out of the city, but they acted like they did not want to leave.

"And while he lingered, the men laid hold upon his hand, and upon the hand of his wife, and upon the hand of his two daughters; the LORD being merciful unto him: and they brought him forth, and set him without the city" (vs. 16). The Lord was being merciful to him, allowing him to get out before the city was destroyed, and he did not even want to leave! The angels grabbed him and his wife and daughters by the hand and dragged them out. They told Lot to run to the mountain. He was afraid to do that. He wanted to go into another city nearby. They told Lot's family to run and not to look back.

"But his wife looked back from behind him, and she became a pillar of salt" (vs. 26). This was the result of the kind of influence that Lot had allowed to take hold of his family. His wife did not only die: she became a pillar of salt.

A. A result of the union of Lot and his own daughter

Lot had lost everything but his two single daughters. He had lost his wife and his married daughters and sons-in-law. He had lost all his material possessions. He was afraid to go to the mountain, but that was where he ended up.

His single daughters decided that they had to do something to preserve the name of their father's family. In those days, it was very important to families to perpetuate the family name. They decided to have an incestual relationship with their father, Lot.

> *"And the firstborn bare a son, and called his name Moab: the same is the father of the Moabites unto this day.*
>
> *"And the younger, she also bare a son, and called his name Benammi: the same is the father of the children of Ammon unto this day."*—Vss. 37, 38.

B. A great-nephew to Abraham, always resentful of the Israelites

What a tragic story! Moab was a result of the union of Lot and his own daughter. So Moab was a great-nephew to Abraham.

We read about Moab again in Numbers 22. The people of Israel were still wandering in the wilderness, and the people of Moab were afraid of them when they got too close: there were so many of them. Balak, the king of Moab, hired Balaam to curse the people of Israel. When he could not convince him to curse them, the Moabites decided to try to defeat the Israelites from the inside out. They started to become friendly with the people of Israel.

> *"And Israel abode in Shittim, and the people began to commit whoredom with the daughters of Moab.*
>
> *"And they called the people unto the sacrifices of their gods: and the people did eat, and bowed down to their gods.*
>
> *"And Israel joined himself unto Baal-peor: and the anger of the LORD was kindled against Israel."*—Num. 25:1–3.

Before the people of Israel ever arrived in the land of Canaan, the people of Moab had already worked to influence them away from the Lord.

Still, God did not allow the people of Israel to fight against the people of Moab, because they had descended from Lot. "And the LORD said unto me [Moses], Distress not the Moabites, neither contend with them in battle: for I will not give thee of their land for a possession; because I have given Ar unto the children of Lot for a possession" (Deut. 2:9).

God was still being merciful to Lot.

The Israelites were in the land of Moab when God spoke to them in Deuteronomy. Before Moses' death and before they went into the Promised Land, the Lord reviewed the Law with them. In Deuteronomy, we read only about the Law; we do not read about oppression from the Moabites. It appears that they left Israel alone during that time. Moses died in the land of Moab at the end of Deuteronomy.

After that, in the Book of Judges, we find Moab oppressing the people of Israel. "And the children of Israel did evil again in the sight of the Lord: and the Lord strengthened Eglon the king of Moab against Israel, because they had done evil in the sight of the Lord" (Judg. 3:12). "So the children of Israel served Eglon the king of Moab eighteen years" (vs. 14).

Then we read about the Israelites worshiping the gods of Moab. By the way, the false god worshiped by the Moabites was Chemosh. Worship of Chemosh included sexual orgies and human sacrifices. "And the children of Israel did evil again in the sight of the LORD, and served Baalim, and Ashtaroth, and the gods of Syria, and the gods of Zidon, and the gods of Moab, and the gods of the children of Ammon, and the gods of the Philistines, and forsook the LORD, and served not him" (10:6).

In Judges 11, the people of Israel wanted only to pass through the land of Moab, but the king of Moab would not allow them to go through.

The relationship that Moab had with the people of Israel is very curious. The reviewing of the Law in Deuteronomy and the end of Moses' life take place in the land of Moab, and the Israelites seem to be undisturbed by the Moabites. At other times, the Moabites are trying to influence the children of Israel to turn from God. Still other times, they are enemies invading the land of Israel.

The Moabites, descendents of Lot, were related to the Israelites, descendents of Abraham. In those days, the people knew their genealogy, and it was important to them to know their lineage. So they knew about the relationship between Abraham and Lot. Besides, Abraham had taken in Lot after his parents died. It was probably because of Abraham that Lot was so wealthy in the first place. Abraham even came to his rescue when he was living in Sodom and was captured.

Actually, it was for Abraham's sake that Lot was saved when Sodom was destroyed. "And it came to pass, when God destroyed the cities of the plain, that God remembered Abraham, and sent Lot out of the midst of the overthrow, when he overthrew the cities in the which Lot dwelt" (Gen. 19:29).

II. God's Ways of Dealing With People

It appears that Lot owed a great debt of gratitude to Abraham, and one would suppose that Lot's descendents would at least be amiable to Israel, knowing from whence they had come. However, it was not so. Why would Moab not be helpful and supportive of the people of Israel? (Actually, there was a time much later when the king of Moab helped David. However, up to the time of Ruth, there did not appear to be a positive relationship between Moab and Israel.)

I have asked why this was so. It appears that Moab, Lot's son (and grandson, by the way), resented his uncle Abraham. Lot had apparently been just as wealthy as Abraham. After Abraham and Lot separated, God continued to bless Abraham in a material way. He continued to be very wealthy.

On the other hand, Lot, who had gone to the world to increase his wealth, ended up losing everything. It did not happen right away. It appears that it took some years before Lot lost it all, but he did lose it eventually.

Moab must have learned at some point in his life that he was the result of an incestual relationship and that Lot had lost all that he had, including most of his family, when the cities were destroyed, while Abraham continued in wealth. Moab was evidently bitter and resentful.

Lest you think I am making this up, the Bible tells us that such will be so. Lot had been a good man as long as he was with Abraham, but he allowed the world to take over in his heart (II Pet. 2:7, 8). He was not doing right; so in that regard, he is the "wicked" in the following verses.

"An unjust man is an abomination to the just: and he that is upright in the way is abomination to the wicked."—Prov. 29:27.

We know that those who do wrong are an abomination to those who want to do right and obey God, but did you realize that the Bible tells us those who do right are detestable to those who do wrong? Perhaps the wrongdoer thinks, *Why does God continue to bless him* [the upright], *while I* [the unjust] *continue to struggle?*

> *"The wicked watcheth the righteous, and seeketh to slay him."*—Ps. 37:32.

Why? Because the righteous makes the wicked look bad. We just talked about when Balak, the king of Moab, tried to get Balaam to curse Israel. When Balak did not succeed in getting Balaam to curse Israel, he decided to infiltrate and get them to turn away from God by initiating personal relationships with them.

> *"The wicked plotteth against the just, and gnasheth upon him with his teeth."*—Vs. 12.

A. For those who love and obey Him, God sends blessings.

Psalm 112:1 says, "Praise ye the LORD. Blessed is the man that feareth the LORD, that delighteth greatly in his commandments." God promises blessings to those who fear Him and who delight greatly in His commandments. What a promise! The next verses describe the blessings that come to those who fear God and delight in His commandments. Then verse 10 says, "The wicked shall see it, and be grieved; he shall gnash with his teeth, and melt away: the desire of the wicked shall perish." It grieves the wicked to see the righteous being blessed by God.

B. Those who choose not to love and obey God will suffer loss.

There is nothing new under the sun. God knows the nature of the human heart and mind. He will bless those who love and obey Him, and those who choose not to love and obey Him will become resentful and bitter.

They could turn to God too, but they often do not make that choice.

After Lot chose to move close to Sodom, God spoke to Abram:

> *"Lift up now thine eyes, and look from the place where thou art northward, and southward, and eastward, and westward:*
>
> *"For all the land which thou seest, to thee will I give it, and to thy seed for ever."* —Gen. 13:14,15.

Abraham continued to receive blessings from God, while Lot lost everything. Lot's descendents were bitter and did what they could to make the people of Israel look bad.

What Lot did in Genesis, Naomi and Elimelech also did in the Book of Ruth. They went to the world (to Moab), hoping to increase their wealth, and they ended up losing everything.

A person who is doing right is blessed by God, while a person who makes terrible choices ends up with his life being a huge mess. He looks at a person who has made excellent choices and obeyed the Lord's commands, and he wonders why that person has been blessed. He resents it. In bitterness, he feels like he has been dealt a raw deal, but his situation is a result of his terrible choices.

A Christian does not have to live that way. If you have been obeying God's commands, ask Him to continue to bless you and then continue to obey, love and serve Him. If you have made terrible choices, start to do right today. God will see it and bless you. Your life may not become calm immediately, because there are natural consequences to poor choices you have already made; but perhaps you can avoid losing everything, as did Lot and Naomi and Elimelech. Even if it seems that you are losing everything, continue to stick with God, and He will bring you through your difficulties if your heart is right before Him.

Keep your heart, mind and delight on God and His Word.

Ruth's Decision

"Intreat me not to leave thee, or to return from following after thee."—Ruth 1:16.

Ruth makes a life-changing decision when her mother-in-law decides to leave the land of Moab and return to the land of Israel. Our hearts are endeared to Ruth as she insists that she leave her homeland and go with Naomi where the future is very uncertain for her.

"And Elimelech Naomi's husband died; and she was left, and her two sons.

"And they took them wives of the women of Moab; the name of the one was Orpah, and the name of the other Ruth: and they dwelled there about ten years.

"And Mahlon and Chilion died also both of them; and the woman was left of her two sons and her husband.

"Then she arose with her daughters in law, that she might return from the country of Moab: for she had heard in the country of Moab how that the LORD had visited his people in giving them bread.

"Wherefore she went forth out of the place where she was, and her two daughters in law with her; and they went on the way to return unto the land of Judah.

"And Naomi said unto her two daughters in law, Go, return each to her mother's house: the LORD deal kindly with you, as ye have dealt with the dead, and with me.

"The LORD grant you that ye may find rest, each of you in the house of her husband. Then she kissed them; and they lifted up their voice, and wept.

"And they said unto her, Surely we will return with thee unto thy people.

"And Naomi said, Turn again, my daughters: why will ye go with me? are there yet any more sons in my womb, that they may be your husbands?

"Turn again, my daughters, go your way; for I am too old to have an husband. If I should say, I have hope, if I should have an husband also to night, and should also bear sons;

"Would ye tarry for them till they were grown? would ye stay for them from having husbands? nay, my daughters; for it grieveth me much for your sakes that the hand of the LORD is gone out against me.

"And they lifted up their voice, and wept again: and Orpah kissed her mother in law; but Ruth clave unto her.

"And she said, Behold, thy sister in law is gone back unto her people, and unto her gods: return thou after thy sister in law.

"And Ruth said, Intreat me not to leave thee, or to return from following after thee: for whither thou goest, I will go; and where thou lodgest, I will lodge: thy people shall be my people, and thy God my God:

"Where thou diest, will I die, and there will I be buried: the LORD do so to me, and more also, if ought but death part thee and me.

"When she saw that she was stedfastly minded to

go with her, then she left speaking unto her.

"So they two went until they came to Beth-lehem. And it came to pass, when they were come to Beth-lehem, that all the city was moved about them, and they said, Is this Naomi?

"And she said unto them, Call me not Naomi, call me Mara: for the Almighty hath dealt very bitterly with me.

"I went out full, and the LORD hath brought me home again empty: why then call ye me Naomi, see-ing the LORD hath testified against me, and the Almighty hath afflicted me?

"So Naomi returned, and Ruth the Moabitess, her daughter in law, with her, which returned out of the country of Moab: and they came to Beth-lehem in the beginning of barley harvest."—1:3–22.

Notice that at first both Orpah and Ruth were deter-mined to go with Naomi (vs. 10). However, Naomi ques-tioned why they would do that (vs. 11). After she asked that question, Naomi reminded Ruth and Orpah that she had no other sons besides the two that those girls had married.

"If brethren dwell together, and one of them die, and have no child, the wife of the dead shall not marry without unto a stranger: her husband's brother shall go in unto her, and take her to him to wife, and perform the duty of an husband's brother unto her.

"And it shall be, that the firstborn which she beareth shall succeed in the name of his brother which is dead, that his name be not put out of Israel."—Deut. 25:5, 6.

It was very important to the people of that time that the name be carried on. These verses teach us that the Lord ordained that if a man die with no children, his brother was to marry his widow; then their firstborn child would carry the name of the brother who had died.

That is why Naomi said to the girls, 'I have no other sons.' Even if she were to get married that very day and have a son right away, surely neither of them would want to wait until that son was old enough to marry him. She was only trying to make the girls be realistic about the situation.

We must remember the state of a widow in those days. The situation looks completely different to us in this day and time. If a woman's husband dies today and she has no means of support, she can get a job. Such was not the case in Naomi's day. A woman did not get a job, and she was destitute. The word *widow* literally means "a desolate place."

Let us ask the question, Why would they return with Naomi? Surely both girls loved Naomi. Naomi told the girls to go back each to her mother's house (vs. 8). Naomi would be destitute, having no husband and no sons; she would not have anything to offer the girls. If they went back to their families, at least they would have houses in which to live. Naomi had no idea what she would have when she returned to the land of Israel.

Naomi appreciated what lovely daughters-in-law Orpah and Ruth had been to her. She prayed that the Lord would be as kind to them as they had been to her and her sons (vs. 8). If the younger widows stayed in Moab, there would be other young men that they could marry. Naomi kissed them and allowed them to go their way (vs. 9). They had helped her carry her possessions part of the way back to Israel and had certainly done more than had been required of them.

They cried some more and kissed and hugged one another some more; then Orpah, as much as she loved Naomi, decided to return to the land of Moab (vs. 14). However, Ruth made a different decision. Her decision was based on much more than a whim or even any sort of selfish desire. She apparently had thought this through very carefully. She appeared to have already been realistic about what she might be facing.

As a matter of fact, Naomi's efforts to dissuade her from going to Israel with her seemed to make her even more determined that she would go. Ruth then insisted that her mother-in-law stop asking her to leave her to go back to Moab: "Intreat me not to leave thee" (vs. 16).

Verses 16 and 17 show us five things that Ruth promised to share with Naomi. These verses are a beautiful testimony of the love of one person for another and are often used in the marriage ceremony. When that is done, these verses are taken out of context; but that does not make them any less appropriate for use in weddings: the promises in these verses are ideal for a bride to pledge to her groom.

I. "Whither thou goest, I will go."

Ruth determined to **go with** Naomi. She was promising to spend her life with Naomi. She must have loved Naomi so very much. There was no husband, only Naomi. By this time, Orpah had decided to return to Moab, so there was not even another young lady with whom to have fellowship in this household. Going with Naomi was going to involve the sharing of the next four things with her.

II. "Where thou lodgest, I will lodge."

Ruth determined to **share** a **home** with Naomi. This

was certainly going to be significant because Naomi was not really promising her that there would be a house in which they could live when they went to Israel. That was one of the things she had brought up to the girls (vs. 8). If they would go back to Moab, they would at least have houses in which to live.

With no husband or sons to take care of her, Naomi had nothing of material value to offer Ruth. Why was she so determined to live with Naomi? Surely she loved her.

However, there is something here of greater drive than that. If it had been only a matter of the love they had for one another, Orpah and Ruth could have easily insisted that Naomi stay with them in Moab where they would have had the families of the girls to help them. We do not read anything in this narrative that suggests that the girls tried to talk Naomi into staying in Moab. Returning to Israel was Naomi's consuming desire.

III. "Thy people shall be my people."

Ruth promised to **share** Naomi's **family and friends** with her. What she was doing here is rather amazing. Ruth was leaving her family and the friends she had known her entire life; she was also leaving all else she had ever known.

If you move to a new area of the country today, you will very likely be able to find banks, grocery stores and shopping malls. You will feel fairly confident that you will be able to locate what you consider to be necessities for your normal routine. Still, it is an adjustment. We may do that for our husbands, but it is our husbands who will provide for us in such moves.

Ruth had no such security. Yet she made a decision

to leave what she knew and go to live with her mother-in-law, where she would have nothing. She was giving up all with which she felt comfortable, assuming that there would be nothing in Israel for her. There they were, two widows with nothing. Ruth certainly did not intend to go for what she could get out of it.

Surely the people of Moab would not admire Ruth for what she was doing; and Ruth must have realized that when she and Naomi would arrive in Israel, the people there would not really trust her at first. They would have to watch her awhile and take some time to get to know her before they would realize that she was a good, loving daughter-in-law to Naomi.

Why would she be willing to make such a move? The answer to that question is found in the next thing that Ruth promised to share with Naomi.

IV. "...Thy God my God."

Ruth promised to **share** Naomi's **faith** with her. I believe this to be the driving force to this entire passage. Ruth had grown up in a land where the god Chemosh was worshiped. Worship of Chemosh involved human sacrifice. It seems completely barbaric to us, but it was all that Ruth had ever known.

Somewhere along the way, Ruth had met the young man Mahlon who had moved to Moab from Israel. He and his family did not believe that Chemosh was the powerful god that the Moabites believed him to be. Ruth learned to know Mahlon and his family. She learned about the almighty God who created the universe. She learned about the power that God had to work in the affairs of life.

Ruth learned to love Mahlon and his mother, whose husband had already passed away. Ruth was impressed with Naomi's wisdom, virtue and grace. Naomi loved Ruth and taught her about the powerful God that she served. Ruth decided to turn her allegiance away from Chemosh to worship the all-knowing, all-powerful, omnipresent God, whose followers did not even have a statue to which to bow down.

Ruth heard the amazing stories of the work of God in the lives of people. She may have heard about the time when God parted the waters of the Red Sea so that the people of Israel could escape from Egypt, and then closed those same waters in on the Egyptian army, killing every soldier. She may have heard that God provided manna in the desert for the entire nation of Israel for forty long years. She may have heard that God parted the waters of the Jordan River so that the people of Israel could enter the land that God had promised them. She may very well have heard that the walls of Jericho fell down flat when the Israelites obeyed God's instructions. She learned that human sacrifice was a barbaric abomination to the almighty God who loves us.

She had no husband, no children, no land, and no money; but she had God. Surely this was the reason that she was so insistent that she stay with Naomi. I believe her real decision was this: "I'm going with you. You know God—the true God." Yes, she loved Naomi, but when she left Moab, she left Chemosh and turned her life over to God.

There was one last thing that Ruth promised to share with Naomi.

V. "Where thou diest, will I die, and there will I be buried."

Even if Naomi would die before Ruth in the land of Israel, Ruth determined she would **stay** there and be buried in that land. Why is this significant? This provides further evidence that the underlying reason for her return was that she was following God. Yes, she loved her mother-in-law; but Ruth determined to stay in the land of Israel where the true God of the universe was worshiped, even after Naomi might die.

Yes, she loved her mother-in-law. Yes, she determined to share home, family and friends with Naomi; but those things would not drive her to stay in Israel after Naomi died. She went there for God.

Ruth made a very important decision that would truly change her life. After she promised to share these things with Naomi, Naomi "left speaking unto her" (vs. 18). That does not mean that she was giving Ruth the "silent treatment." It means that she stopped trying to persuade her to stay in Moab after she heard her determination in this whole matter.

This is truly a lovely story, and it vividly illustrates Ruth's admirable intentions to turn her life over to God. However, how can we apply this passage to us?

We can see that Ruth left all that she knew and turned her life over to God. She left her family and friends. They continued to worship Chemosh. After Naomi and Ruth left Moab, life there probably continued on much the same as it had been. Ruth's family and friends may have already gravitated away from her before she moved. She had changed. She was no longer interested in the things that had formerly interested her.

A similar thing is true today: if you stop doing what

your friends do, you will not have to leave them; they will leave you. This brings us to a very real reason that it is so difficult for someone today to leave his sinful lifestyle and turn his life over to God. In order to do that, one may have to leave his family and/or friends.

Consider, if you will, a person who is involved in alcohol. His life is a mess, but he does not know how to fix it. He has made many terrible decisions that have gotten him into the situation in which he finds himself. He may come to church, looking for a way to improve his life. He hears about how the Lord can save his soul and give him a home in Heaven. It all sounds so wonderful. At church he sees happy, vibrant Christians who love God and live a pleasant life.

However, after a soul winner leads him to the Lord at church, he goes home. There are drinks in the refrigerator. The next day he goes to work. His friend calls him and wants to meet him after work for a drink. It is what they have done for many years. After the drink, he goes home and has wine with his dinner and then relaxes in the family room with a beer. Friday night he goes to a party and has too much to drink. An unpleasant scene follows, and he ends up hitting his wife. Saturday night he meets his friends at the bar and has too much to drink. He sees red and blue flashing lights in his rearview mirror on the way home, which are immediately followed by a DUI citation.

He thinks, *How is this possible? What is going on here? How could this happen? I went to church! I prayed and asked God to save me! Why isn't He blessing me like He blesses those people that I met at church?*

Going to church is a wonderful thing to do, and getting saved is the very best thing a person can ever do; but those things alone will not change a person's present situation if he does not change the things he does. The Lord will bless a Christian as he obeys and serves Him. There are consequences to choices. If a new convert continues to make the same choices he made before he got saved, he will experience the same consequences.

If you continue to do the same things, you will get the same results. If you want your life to change, you must change the things you do.

Ruth left her family and friends and determined to go with Naomi who had influenced her in the direction of love and service to God. Ruth left Chemosh.

Above we gave an example of a man who had an alcohol problem. If that man's life is going to change, he is going to have to get rid of the alcohol that had been his god. Ruth learned to love the Lord, and she determined not to go back to Chemosh. That was why she told Naomi that she would die in the land of Israel. Ruth changed her mind and thereby allowed God to work in her heart and effect change in her life.

Do you want your life to change? You have to change the way you live. You have to change what you do. Blessing comes only from God. Love Him, obey Him, serve Him, and learn His Word.

Do you have a friend who wants his life to change? Encourage him to change his life, but he will have to be willing to change what he does. Blessing comes only from God. Encourage your friend to love Him, obey Him, serve Him, and learn His Word.

God can change your life, but you have to turn it over to Him. He can't change your life if you continue to control it yourself by making terrible choices. It seems strange to say that God *cannot* do something. Perhaps we should say that He *won't* change your life if you continue to control it by making terrible choices. Remember, God does not *force* Himself on us; He *offers*. The blessings are ours if we want them. Do you want them?

We looked at Psalm 37:1–3 in the first chapter of *Gleanings From Ruth*. In those verses, we learned that we must not worry about what appears to be prosperity in the lives of those who do not do right. They have already received their reward, while those who obey God have a greater blessing coming to them as they trust the Lord. In this chapter we have seen the truth of Psalm 37:5, which says, "Commit thy way unto the LORD; trust also in him; and he shall bring it to pass."

Committing your way to the Lord means to turn everything over to Him. Turn your life over to God and simply trust Him; then He will bring it to pass. He will bring what to pass? We have no idea! Whatever it is, it will be great because it comes from God.

At this point in the story, Ruth has not seen God "bring it to pass," but she has committed her way to Him. We can read the end of the story and find that God did greatly bless Ruth's life; but at the time she chose to go to Israel, she had no clue what blessings were in store for her due to the fact that she had committed her life to the Lord.

You cannot see the end of your story either, just as Ruth could not see the end for herself. You have no clue what blessings are in store for you if you will just commit your life into the Lord's hands. None of us know what the Lord can do with us and for us.

The message for us from this lesson is simple. Do what Ruth did. Give your life to God. If there is something in your life that you need to leave in order to go to God, leave it and go to God. Many things in life are beyond your control, but one thing you can do is to give yourself to God.

Orpah's Decision

"Behold, thy sister in law [Orpah] is gone back unto her people, and unto her gods."—Ruth 1:15.

In the previous chapter, we looked at the decision Ruth made to follow her mother-in-law to the land of Israel. She left all that she had ever known to go to Israel where she would very likely have nothing of material value to her name. We looked at the promises Ruth made to Naomi and concluded that the underlying reason she decided to leave Moab to go to Israel was that she had learned about the almighty God, the Creator of the universe, and was willing to leave her home where the false god, Chemosh, was being worshiped through human sacrifice.

In this chapter we will look at what Orpah decided to do when faced with the same information that Ruth had. Orpah's decision was very different from the one Ruth made.

We find the name of Orpah only twice in the Bible, and both times it is here in Ruth 1—once in verse 4 and once in verse 14. We do not know very much about her, because when she left Naomi, that is the last we hear of her. The Bible mentions her no more.

Verse 6 tells us that *both* Ruth and Orpah arose with Naomi to return to the land of Israel. So Orpah had initially decided to go with Naomi. Verse 8 tells us that *both* Ruth and Orpah had been kind and loving to Naomi. In verse 9, we see that *both* girls kissed Naomi and wept at the thought of leaving her. We see in verse 10 that *both* girls said, "Surely we will return with thee unto thy people."

However, after Naomi presented the cold, hard reality of the situation in the next three verses, suddenly Orpah kissed her mother-in-law and left her, in order to stay in Moab (vs. 14).

What can we learn from the difference in the girls' decisions in this passage? Why did Orpah decide to return to Moab, while Ruth did not? It appears that she had the same love for Naomi as Ruth did. The answer can be found in the reason for Ruth's decision. She left Moab to go to God. Orpah did not.

The previous chapter of this book discusses the fact that if you want change in your life, you must decide to do things differently. That was what Ruth did. Orpah made no such change. Surely she had learned about the God of the Israelites just as Ruth had. When she returned to Moab, she returned to the worship of Chemosh.

Could Orpah have continued to worship God in the land of Moab? Even if she was the only one there who was doing so, could she still devote her life to God? Probably not.

You can ask the same question today: "Can't I be a good Christian and not go to church?" I would say that you can be *saved* and not go to church. However, the term *Christian* means that you act like Christ would act. It means that you are a follower of Christ. Without the fellowship and encouragement of others who love the Lord and serve Him, and without reading the Bible and praying, you will easily drift away. Then you will not be following Christ. Without listening to the preaching of God's Word, you will forget even what you once knew. It will be easy to stop reading the Bible and to stop praying, and it will be easy to slip into whatever activities are taking place around you, even if you know they are not good for you.

I suggest that you really cannot be a good Christian without going to church, because you have to stick with God. You have to stay close; you have to keep your mind and heart on the Lord. Do not ever let yourself get away from Him.

I would say that it would be very unlikely that Orpah continued in devotion to the Lord in the land of Moab.

What accounts for the difference between the decisions of the two girls? The answer to that question can be found in one of the parables that Jesus told.

> *"Hearken; Behold, there went out a sower to sow:*
>
> *"And it came to pass, as he sowed, some fell by the way side, and the fowls of the air came and devoured it up.*
>
> *"And some fell on stony ground, where it had not much earth; and immediately it sprang up, because it had no depth of earth:*
>
> *"But when the sun was up, it was scorched; and because it had no root, it withered away.*
>
> *"And some fell among thorns, and the thorns grew up, and choked it, and it yielded no fruit.*

"And other fell on good ground, and did yield fruit that sprang up and increased; and brought forth, some thirty, and some sixty, and some an hundred."—Mark 4:3–8.

Jesus explained the parable in the verses to follow.

"The sower soweth the word.

"And these are they by the way side, where the word is sown; but when they have heard, Satan cometh immediately, and taketh away the word that was sown in their hearts.

"And these are they likewise which are sown on stony ground; who, when they have heard the word, immediately receive it with gladness;

"And have no root in themselves, and so endure but for a time: afterward, when affliction or persecution ariseth for the word's sake, immediately they are offended.

"And these are they which are sown among thorns; such as hear the word,

"And the cares of this world, and the deceitfulness of riches, and the lusts of other things entering in, choke the word, and it becometh unfruitful.

"And these are they which are sown on good ground; such as hear the word, and receive it, and bring forth fruit, some thirtyfold, some sixty, and some an hundred."—Vss. 14–20.

Ruth and Orpah had the same environment, and they were responding to the same information. What caused them to make different choices? The answer to that question is fairly simple: it depends on the condition of one's heart. It is the same reason that any one of us will make one decision or another, especially regarding spiritual things.

In the parable of the sower, the seed is the same in all cases. It is the Word of God. All the seed was good seed; the difference is in the ground. The Word of God is the same for everyone; the difference is in the hearts of the people who hear it.

Ruth is a picture of the good ground that received the seed sown. Her heart was softened as she learned about God, and she believed in Him. She wanted to leave the life of human sacrifice to the false god, Chemosh, and turn her life over to God. She wanted to leave Moab and go to a place where the people believed in and served the almighty God.

I think Orpah's response to the amount of spiritual light she was given is a picture of the thorns that choked the seed. "The cares of this world" might have been an attitude that said, "If I stay in Moab, I will be able to find a husband again."

"The deceitfulness of riches" might have led her to say, "If I stay in Moab, I will have a house to live in with my family."

"The lusts of other things" might have made her wonder, *Moab is all I've ever known. Will it really be better to leave and go to a place where the future is so uncertain? We are just three widows wondering what to do.*

These thoughts and attitudes that Orpah might have had, "entering in," may have "choke[d] the word."

Ruth received the Word—that is, she took it in. She wanted all the blessings from the Lord that were available to her. She was willing to leave that with which she was comfortable in order to get closer to God.

Sometimes even though our situation is not good, we

do not want to leave what we know in order to get closer to God. Doing so would require us to leave that with which we are comfortable, and it would require us to trust God. If we have never trusted God before, we do not know what it would be like to do so. Orpah was apparently comfortable even in Moab. We can allow ourselves to stay in a hole into which we have dug ourselves, because we are familiar with that hole and we know how to operate there. We know it is uncomfortable, we know it is difficult, and we see other people who do not live like we are living; but we are unfamiliar with what it might be like outside our hole.

You may be asking, *Okay, how do I get out of where I am?* I do not know the specifics of your circumstance; but I know that the answer is to draw closer to God, learn His Word and obey Him, stay in church, stay in close fellowship with other believers, and trust God. It sounds hard to believe; it sounds like I am not facing the reality of life. Dear reader, God *is* reality. God's blessings are real!

Do you believe God's Word? I hope you do.

> *"Blessed are the undefiled in the way, who walk in the law of the LORD.*
>
> *"Blessed are they that keep his testimonies, and that seek him with the whole heart."* —Ps. 119:1, 2.

Do you want God to bless you? Walk in the law of the Lord. Seek Him with your whole heart.

> *"Wherewithal shall a young man cleanse his way? by taking heed thereto according to thy word.*
>
> *"With my whole heart have I sought thee: O let me not wander from thy commandments."* —Vss. 9, 10.

Do you want your way to be cleansed? Take heed to

God's Word. That means listen and obey.

David wrote many of the psalms. He knew how easy it was to wander away from God. He asked God not to *let* him wander away from His commandments. God has some interesting ways of getting our attention, and David was willing to risk having God "turn up the heat" or "beat him up" somehow for the sake of keeping his heart right with God.

"Blessed is the man that feareth the LORD, that delighteth greatly in his commandments" (112:1). Do you want God to bless you? Fear Him and delight in His commandments.

> "The steps of a good man are ordered by the LORD: and he delighteth in his way.
>
> "Though he fall, he shall not be utterly cast down: for the LORD upholdeth him with his hand."— 37:23, 24.

If you obey God, your steps will be ordered by the Lord; and even if you have a problem and fall, God will uphold you with His hand.

When we studied Ruth's decision, we looked at Psalm 37:5, which says, "Commit thy way unto the LORD; trust also in him; and he shall bring it to pass." Remember that this comes after verse 4, which says, "Delight thyself also in the LORD; and he shall give thee the desires of thine heart." If you delight in the Lord, your desires will be His desires. Turn your life over to God and trust Him, and He will order your life.

> "Trust in the LORD with all thine heart; and lean not unto thine own understanding.
>
> "In all thy ways acknowledge him, and he shall direct thy paths.

"Be not wise in thine own eyes: fear the LORD, and depart from evil."

"Favour is deceitful, and beauty is vain: but a woman that feareth the LORD, she shall be praised."—Prov. 3:5–7; 31:30.

If we could get this straight in our lives, most of the things that we talk about and fret about would take care of themselves.

"Trust in the LORD." Do what He says. He knows what He is talking about.

"Lean not unto thine own understanding." Don't try to figure things out; just trust God.

"Acknowledge him." Make all your decisions based on what God would want.

"He shall direct thy paths." God will work in the circumstances of your life to lead you where He wants you to go in order to fulfill His will.

"Fear the LORD, and depart from evil." Sometimes the decision is so simple. Just avoid doing wrong.

Maybe it did not make sense to Orpah to go to Israel. Ruth went because of God. She was acknowledging Him (Prov. 3:6). Orpah was not looking only to God. She did not fear Him, and she did not depart from evil (vs. 7).

If any of those things will come true—if the Lord is going to bless you, if He will direct your way—then you have to delight in the Lord, trust Him, fear Him, turn your life over to Him, take heed to His Word, and seek Him with your whole heart. Give yourself to God.

"What doth the LORD thy God require of thee, but to fear the LORD thy God, to walk in all his ways,

and to love him, and to serve the LORD *thy God with all thy heart and with all thy soul,*

"To keep the commandments of the LORD, *and his statutes, which I command thee this day for thy good?"*—Deut. 10:12, 13.

It is for your own good to give your heart to God and obey and serve Him.

"Master, which is the great commandment in the law?

"Jesus said unto him, Thou shalt love the Lord thy God with all thy heart, and with all thy soul, and with all thy mind."—Matt. 22:36, 37.

There are many verses that teach us the same things. Give the Lord your heart. Love Him. If you love Him, you will obey Him.

Did Orpah live a terrible life when she went back to Moab? Probably not, but she turned away from God and went back to the world. She had heard the same message that Ruth did, but she decided to turn back.

Orpah made the same decision that Lot, the ancestor of the Moabites, had made. When he had a choice, he chose to move toward the world. He knew about God, but he let the world come in. We all remember what happened to him.

One day Orpah died. She stood before God. Can you see God looking at her? "Orpah, you heard the message about the one true God of the universe, and then you went back to the false god, Chemosh. Not good, Orpah."

Someday we all will die and stand before God. Is He going to be pleased with how you and I responded to what we knew about His Word? It is a very sobering thought.

> "For if after they have escaped the pollutions of the world through the knowledge of the Lord and Saviour Jesus Christ, they are again entangled therein, and overcome, the latter end is worse with them than the beginning.
>
> "For it had been better for them not to have known the way of righteousness, than, after they have known it, to turn from the holy commandment delivered unto them."—II Pet. 2:20, 21.

Orpah knew about God, but she turned away.

If we fear God in this life, we will not have to be afraid of Him in the next life.

Let us learn a valuable lesson from both Ruth and Orpah. It is the same lesson, but we see it from opposite sides. Ruth left godlessness and gave her life to God. He greatly blessed her. Orpah went back to the godlessness. Do not follow her example. Follow Ruth's example. Stay with God.

Who Was Boaz?

"The LORD recompense thy work, and a full reward be given thee of the LORD God of Israel, under whose wings thou art come to trust."—Ruth 2:12.

In Ruth, chapter 1, we saw that Naomi and Elimelech went to Moab to escape a famine in Israel. In Moab, Elimelech died, and Naomi was left with her two sons. They each married a young lady from Moab; then the two boys died. Naomi, a widow, had two daughters-in-law, both widows. They had no means of support, but Naomi heard that the famine in Israel was over. After having lived in Moab for ten years, she decided to return to the land of Israel.

Ruth and Orpah, Naomi's two daughters-in-law, intended to go with her. Both of them did go part of the way with her. However, after Naomi made the situation clear to them, Orpah decided to stay in Moab, but Ruth was determined to stay with Naomi so that she could continue to follow God. Naomi and Ruth returned to Bethlehem in the beginning of barley harvest (1:22).

The next verse introduces another character to the story: "And Naomi had a kinsman of her husband's, a mighty man of wealth, of the family of Elimelech; and his name was Boaz" (Ruth 2:1).

In this chapter of our study we investigate who Boaz was. This verse says he was a wealthy man and he was related to Naomi's late husband, Elimelech. There is more to learn about Boaz.

We can learn a valuable lesson by looking at Boaz's parentage. The name Boaz appears in the Bible only a small number of times outside the Book of Ruth. It appears in I Chronicles 2:11, 12; in Matthew 1:5; and in Luke 3:32—all in the genealogy listings. Then his name appears in II Chronicles 3:17 and in I Kings 7:21, where we read that one of the pillars in Solomon's temple was named Boaz.

The pillar in the temple was named Boaz to signify "In Him Is Strength." What a wonderful name for a mother to give to her son!

The genealogies in Matthew and Luke were recorded to prove to us that Jesus came from the line of David. Among the listings we read: "And Salmon begat Booz of Rachab; and Booz begat Obed of Ruth; and Obed begat Jesse" (Matt. 1:5). "[David] was the son of Jesse, which was the son of Obed, which was the son of Booz, which was the son of Salmon" (Luke 3:32).

Matthew told us that Salmon begat Boaz of Rahab. It is interesting to notice that only four women are mentioned in the genealogy of Christ in Matthew, and Rahab, the mother of Boaz, is one of them. Each of those four women has an interesting story and a lesson for us. In this chapter we will talk only about Rahab, the mother of Boaz.

Joshua 2 tells us who Rahab was. "And Joshua the son of Nun sent out of Shittim two men to spy secretly, saying, Go view the land, even Jericho. And they went, and came into an harlot's house, named Rahab, and lodged there" (vs. 1). In this verse, we learn that Rahab was a harlot, a prostitute, and that she was living in the city of Jericho. The people of Jericho did not worship God, and that was why the people of Israel were told to defeat them.

"And she said unto the men, I know that the LORD hath given you the land" (vs. 9).

Rahab was from Jericho. She had not learned about the almighty God who created the universe, but she had heard some amazing things about the God of the Israelites, and we know the God of the Israelites was indeed the almighty Creator.

The rest of verse 9 continues, "Your terror is fallen upon us, and that all the inhabitants of the land faint because of you." She knew there was something special about those Israelites, and she was not the only one who was convinced that God had given the people of Israel the land on which she was standing. All the inhabitants of that place were terrified to know that the people of Israel were coming. Why was this so?

"For we have heard how the LORD dried up the water of the Red sea for you, when ye came out of Egypt" (vs. 10). It is astounding to know that the heathen people of Jericho, who did not trust God, believed that it was the God of the Israelites who had opened the water of the Red Sea for them. It is equally astounding to me that they were still talking about it and were fearful because of it after *forty years* had gone by. Remember that the people of Israel had been in the wilderness for forty years.

Rahab continues, "...and what ye did unto the two

kings of the Amorites, that were on the other side Jordan, Sihon and Og, whom ye utterly destroyed" (vs. 10). The people of Jericho knew that the Israelites had destroyed those two nations, and they were terrified to know that they were the next target. The city of Jericho had high, wide, strong walls which they considered to be impenetrable. Inside those walls, they felt completely safe until they realized that the people of Israel were on their way and that their God was more powerful than any other god about whom they had ever heard.

When Rahab saw those two men coming into the city and realized that they were Israelites, she saw her chance to move over to the winning side. She hid those men on the roof of her house. When the king sent servants looking for the spies, Rahab stood boldly before them and lied to their faces. She told them that the men had been there but that she did not know who they were, and that they had left. She said that the men went out just before the gate was shut, and she was certain that the soldiers could overtake them, because it had not been very long since they had left.

After the soldiers left her house, she returned to the roof where she had hidden the spies. She asked them to have kindness shown to her because she had shown kindness to them in hiding them. She asked them to agree to save her life and the lives of the family members she had in her home when the Israelites returned to destroy their city. She was convinced that the city of Jericho would be destroyed at the hands of the Israelites, because she believed that God was in control.

"And as soon as we had heard these things [the Red Sea dried up; those two kings were defeated on the other side of the Jordan River], our hearts did melt, neither did there remain any more courage in any man, because of you: for the LORD your God, he is God in heaven above, and in earth beneath" (vs. 11). Rahab may have been a heathen, and she may have been a prostitute, but she believed God. She really did not understand what it meant yet to believe God, but she believed as much as she knew.

When the people of Israel returned to defeat the city of Jericho, the spies went into her house and rescued her and her family. They went to live with the Israelites. "And Joshua saved Rahab the harlot alive, and her father's household, and all that she had; and she dwelleth in Israel even unto this day; because she hid the messengers, which Joshua sent to spy out Jericho" (6:25).

The historical narrative in the next books of the Bible does not record any more information about Rahab and her family. However, we find her name included in the genealogy of Matthew 1, showing that she was in the family line leading to Jesus. This shows us that one of the Israelites married her. Imagine that an Israelite would marry a heathen woman who had been a prostitute!

We also find the name of Rahab in Hebrews 11. We know this chapter as the list of the faithful. Verse 31 says, "By faith the harlot Rahab perished not with them that believed not, when she had received the spies with peace."

According to that verse, Rahab survived the battle at Jericho because she believed God. She did not die with those who did not believe. She had been a heathen, an idol-worshiper and a harlot; but she turned to God and believed on Him. God blessed her.

Joshua saved her because she protected the spies. God saved her because she believed in Him. You may have wonderful things happen to you because of the work of other people; but make no mistake—the blessings come from God (though through those people) because of your faith in Him.

She was saved from the battle and taken to live with the Israelites. She knew nothing of God but what she had heard that He had done for the people of Israel. She did not know how God was to be worshiped. She did not know God's Word. She had not learned God's dietary laws or the commandments of God regarding how to live together and treat others. All she knew was that she believed that God was in control—that He was more powerful than the gods that she had been taught to worship. She was convinced that the people of Israel would defeat Jericho because God was on their side, even though the citizens of Jericho had always felt completely safe in such a strongly fortified city. She did not know anything but that she believed God would win.

She must have believed truly and very strongly that God would win that battle. Imagine, if you will, what Rahab's situation would have been if the people of Israel had not won that battle and all the people of Jericho had lived. Remember that she had invited her family to be with her in her house. After the battle was over, surely everyone would have been talking about it. Eventually the word would have gotten out that Rahab had protected the spies from Israel and had made an agreement with them. She could have been killed for treason or at least blackballed somehow by her people. If Jericho had won, it would have been very bad for her. She believed God was in control.

I have often wondered if the people of Israel welcomed Rahab, if they encouraged her, if they talked to her and helped her learn how to live among them, or if they looked at her suspiciously and warned their children to stay away from her. I have often wondered if the people were encouraged by the great faith that Rahab had in the power of God, even without knowing God's Word, or if they pointed their finger at her ignorance of the things of God.

According to the genealogy in Matthew 1, a man named Salmon of the tribe of Judah married Rahab (vs. 5). It appears, then, that somebody thought she was special. According to Hebrews 11:31, she is one of the people that God thought should be included in the list of those who had such great faith that He presents them to us as examples. So we see that God thought she was very special.

This was the mother of Boaz. Rahab was a sinner saved by the grace of God. So are you; so am I. If we see such persons walk through the doors of our churches, we ought to welcome, love and encourage them. We do not know what God can do with them.

Before I understood who Boaz's mother was, I wondered why Boaz would have married a non-Jew from Moab. She had not grown up with the people of Israel, and she had learned many customs contrary to those in Israel among God's people. In Ruth 2, Boaz is presented as a fine, upstanding man of Israel. It did not make sense to me that he would marry Ruth. However, when I realized that Rahab was his mother, the picture for me changed completely. As we study Ruth 2, we see that Boaz looked at Ruth's soundness of character and her willingness to follow God even to a foreign place.

Boaz said, "It hath fully been shewed me, all that thou

hast done unto thy mother in law since the death of thine husband: and how thou hast left thy father and thy mother, and the land of thy nativity, and art come unto a people which thou knewest not heretofore" (vs. 11).

Boaz even prayed for God's blessings on Ruth's life because she had determined to follow God. "The LORD recompense thy work, and a full reward be given thee of the LORD God of Israel, under whose wings thou art come to trust" (vs. 12).

Boaz had seen firsthand in his own mother's life what God could do with a woman who trusted Him, even though she had not been reared among God's people and she knew nothing of God except what she had heard that He had done for His own.

I am so thankful that God's requirements for blessing do not include proper upbringing. God's requirements for blessing include a personal decision to believe Him, trust Him, love Him, obey Him, serve Him, and learn His Word. Even if you did not grow up in the "right" kind of family, you can make your own decision to follow the Lord.

Perhaps you grew up in a Christian home where the Word of God was preeminent; that is, it was the only source of truth. However, you may have grown up with no knowledge of the Lord and His Word. Beginning today, let that make no difference in your walk with the Lord.

You can no longer blame your parents or your siblings for what you decided to do with your life. You cannot stand before God and say, "Well, my dad was a drunk, and so I drink; it's all his fault"; or, "My dad disobeyed everything, and I am just like him"; or, "My parents did not love me or train me right, so that's just how

I am." That will hold no weight with God.

You can decide to follow, believe and trust God, despite your upbringing. You can learn His Word even if you knew nothing about it as you grew up. The decision is yours to make. God will hold you accountable for your faith in Him or the lack thereof.

Even if you did grow up in a good Christian family, knowing God and His Word, you still have to make your own decision to obey Him. The good character of your parents does not cause God to be pleased with you. Whether or not you will obey God is a decision you must make, and God will hold you accountable for your faith in Him or the lack thereof.

Boaz saw what God was able to do with his mother because she believed Him. Boaz looked at Ruth and saw that she trusted and believed God. He saw soundness of character. He was impressed.

At this point in the lives of Boaz and Ruth, they did not know that they would be married; they did not know that they would have a child; they did not know that they would be part of the genealogy of Christ; but Boaz knew his mother, and he was learning to know Ruth. Both women had left all they had known in order to follow God. Boaz had already seen how God had blessed his mother. It appeared to him that Ruth was another such lady who would follow God.

You can decide to follow Him too. Decide today to believe, trust and obey God.

Ruth Serving; God Providing

"They that seek the LORD shall not want any good thing."—Ps. 34:10.

In the beginning of Ruth, chapter 2, we were introduced to Boaz. In the previous chapter of our study, we took a good look at who Boaz was. We saw that his own mother was not necessarily the kind of woman you would expect to be held in high esteem in the Scriptures, but that she believed what she knew of God even when she knew very little. All she knew was that God was in control and that He was powerful enough to defeat anyone, even the people in a strongly fortified city such as Jericho.

In this chapter we turn our attention back to Ruth. After traveling to Bethlehem, Ruth set out to serve her mother-in-law. Because of her sweet and kind spirit and her servant's attitude, God blessed her and provided for her. As we look at the events in chapter 2 and parallel those with our own service to God, we can see how He will provide for us if we are willing to serve Him.

We must remember that the chapter divisions in the Bible were added later, after the narrative was written. Chapter 1 flows directly into chapter 2. We are given a few pieces of information here. We saw in Ruth 1:22 that

Naomi and Ruth returned to Bethlehem at the beginning of barley harvest. In Ruth 2:1 we are introduced to Boaz. He was related to Elimelech, and he was wealthy.

Now we see Ruth seeking sustenance for Naomi and herself. "And Ruth the Moabitess said unto Naomi, Let me now go to the field, and glean ears of corn after him in whose sight I shall find grace. And she said unto her, Go, my daughter" (vs. 2). Ruth asked Naomi if she would be permitted to see if she could find someone who would allow her to glean in his fields as the reapers were working.

In the next verses, those pieces of information are used to continue the narrative.

The Law of God provides for the support of the poor in this practice of gleaning.

> "And when ye reap the harvest of your land, thou shalt not wholly reap the corners of thy field, neither shalt thou gather the gleanings of thy harvest.
>
> "And thou shalt not glean thy vineyard, neither shalt thou gather every grape of thy vineyard; thou shalt leave them for the poor and stranger: I am the LORD your God."
>
> "And when ye reap the harvest of your land, thou shalt not make clean riddance of the corners of thy field when thou reapest, neither shalt thou gather any gleaning of thy harvest: thou shalt leave them unto the poor, and to the stranger: I am the Lord your God."—Lev. 19:9,10; 23:22.
>
> "When thou gatherest the grapes of thy vineyard, thou shalt not glean it afterward: it shall be for the stranger, for the fatherless, and for the widow."—Deut. 24:21.

Notice in those verses that God understood that there would be poor people in the land of Israel. He provided for them in such a way that they could obtain what they needed, but they still had some personal responsibility for it. He provides for the poor, not the lazy. Remember that when God sent manna to the people of Israel in the wilderness, they still had to go out and pick it up. If God could send enough manna to supply the needs of all those people in the wilderness, He could just as capably put it in bowls in their tents. He did not do that, however: they still had to gather it for themselves.

He instructed those with lands and crops to reap and not to work too hard at gathering every little bit of the crop. He ended both of the verses in Leviticus by reminding His people, "I am the LORD your God." He is merciful to us; we ought to be merciful to the poor. What we leave for the poor should not be considered a loss, but a mercy to those who do not have enough. Besides, He says, "I am the LORD your God." If you obey God and allow the poor to use what you have grown, God will bless you. He will take care of your needs if you are willing to help those with less.

Still, it appears that perhaps some did not practice this merciful act of leaving gleanings for the poor. Ruth said she would look for someone "in whose sight I shall find grace." Perhaps she was afraid that some would not allow her to glean because they would learn that she was not of the people of Israel, but of Moab.

In any case, she did not know anyone, and she simply went out looking for a field that was being harvested where she could glean. "And she went, and came, and gleaned in the field after the reapers: and her hap was to light on a part of the field belonging unto Boaz, who was of the kindred of Elimelech" (Ruth 2:3).

This is so exciting. "Her hap" means that she went out and just happened to come across the field belonging to Boaz, who was related to Naomi and was very wealthy. He was also the son of Rahab, that previously heathen woman from Jericho who had grown to have such great faith in God that she is presented as an example to us today. Ruth did not know anything about Boaz; she just happened upon his field. This is obviously the hand of God at work. When the Lord is at work, nothing is an accident.

We are going to see that as Ruth worked in an attitude of service, God provided for her in ways that she had probably never considered. At this point in the narrative, the information is provided, the stage is set, and the Lord moves on with the narrative.

In verse 4, "Boaz came from Beth-lehem, and said unto the reapers, The LORD be with you. And they answered him, The LORD bless thee." Boaz was kind and encouraging to his workers. He greeted them in a kind manner. He did not sound like he was going to berate them. Perhaps he was making sure the work was moving forward and checking on the workers' well-being.

Just as Boaz was kind and encouraging to his servants, God blesses those who serve Him. It sounds as though Boaz was asking if there was anything they needed or if he could do anything for them. God wants to do for us what we need. "For the eyes of the LORD run to and fro throughout the whole earth, to shew himself strong in the behalf of them whose heart is perfect toward him" (II Chron. 16:9). God is looking to bless those who love Him!

"Then said Boaz unto his servant that was set over the reapers, Whose damsel is this?" (Ruth 2:5). Boaz had one servant who was there to oversee the work of the other servants. In his absence, Boaz left someone in charge.

In a similar way, God sets some of His servants in a position of leadership in the work of His ministry. This does not make those people better than other Christians; it means only that they have a different responsibility. Someone has to be in charge, or the work does not move forward.

Boaz asked who Ruth was. This shows that he was interested in people and not only the work. She was "only" a gleaner. He could have felt that he did not have to know who she was or anything about her. He could have felt that he did not even need to know anything about her circumstances or why she felt that she had to come to glean. She was really of no consequence to such a wealthy man, but Boaz was interested in her as a person nonetheless. He wondered who she was.

"And the servant that was set over the reapers answered and said, It is the Moabitish damsel that came back with Naomi out of the country of Moab" (vs. 6). Apparently everyone had heard about this young lady. Notice that the servant was working, and he was responsible to answer to Boaz for how the work was progressing and for who was there. The people whom God places in a leadership role within the ministry will answer to God for what they have done and how they have served God and others.

"And she said, I pray you, let me glean and gather after the reapers among the sheaves: so she came, and hath continued even from the morning until now, that she tarried a little in the house" (vs. 7). He reported to Boaz that she had asked permission before she started to glean and that she had been working hard with only a small break.

Boaz was pleased with what he heard. He approached Ruth and told her that she was welcome to stay right there and did not need to think about going to anyone else's field to glean.

> *"Then said Boaz unto Ruth, Hearest thou not, my daughter? Go not to glean in another field, neither go from hence, but abide here fast by my maidens:*
>
> *"Let thine eyes be on the field that they do reap, and go thou after them: have I not charged the young men that they shall not touch thee? and when thou art athirst, go unto the vessels, and drink of that which the young men have drawn."*—Vss. 8, 9.

Boaz was making sure Ruth understood that she need not worry about where she would get food. She was welcome to continue to glean in his fields. Notice that he provided for her to obtain what she needed, but he made no suggestion that he would give her grain outright. She still had to gather it. He kindly offered for her to stay by his young ladies that were working so that she would not be among the men. He promised her that the men would be respectful to her. He offered her water to drink from the water that was already drawn—thus being more gracious than if he had told her merely from where she could draw water.

Ruth was very thankful. She had offered to serve Naomi, providing for her needs, and now her needs were being met. Actually it sounds as though she could hardly believe someone would be so kind to her (and she had not even heard all that Boaz would do for her).

We see her response: "Then she fell on her face, and bowed herself to the ground, and said unto him, Why have I found grace in thine eyes, that thou shouldest take knowledge of me, seeing I am a stranger?" (vs. 10).

His answer to her shows us that he was very impressed with what he had heard about Ruth. Perhaps already he could see a parallel to his own mother.

> *"And Boaz answered and said unto her, It hath fully been shewed me, all that thou hast done unto thy mother in law since the death of thine husband: and how thou hast left thy father and thy mother, and the land of thy nativity, and art come unto a people which thou knewest not heretofore.*
>
> *"The Lord recompense thy work, and a full reward be given thee of the Lord God of Israel, under whose wings thou art come to trust.*
>
> *"Then she said, Let me find favour in thy sight, my lord; for that thou hast comforted me, and for that thou hast spoken friendly unto thine handmaid, though I be not like unto one of thine handmaidens."—Vss. 11–13.*

Notice that she did not consider herself to be like one of his maidens. I have wondered why she thought this. She was a stranger, she was not a Jew, she had only recently learned about God, but was she different from them? Not really.

When I first walked into a church, I thought I saw radiant Christians who knew and loved the Lord. I thought I saw people who knew the Bible thoroughly and trusted God completely. I knew I was not one of those, and I did not know how to be one of those, but that was what I wanted to be.

I used to think that I was the only one who thought these kinds of things. However, as I grew in knowing the Lord, I realized that many of us wonder the same things, though perhaps all of us think that we are the only ones wondering such.

1. Do you feel that you will never measure up to others in your spiritual walk?

2. Do you feel that you will never be the same kind of vibrant Christian as someone else you may look up to?

3. Do you wish that you knew the Bible as thoroughly as someone else you may know?

None of that matters!

First of all, you do not have to measure up to someone else. In your walk with the Lord, what someone else is does not matter. Your walk with the Lord is between you and God. We are each in a different place in our relationship with the Lord. I need to continue to grow closer to Him. It is foolish to compare myself with someone else. In doing so, my eyes are on that person and not on God. I need to focus on God and His Word.

Second, whether or not you are a vibrant Christian is between you and the Lord. You can look to others for encouragement and teaching, but you do not have to measure yourself by someone else.

Third, whether or not you learn to know the Bible is between you and the Lord. You can listen to others for teaching, but the only way for you to learn the Bible is to stay in the Book.

Surely you can see a pattern here. You do not have

to measure yourself by what others do. Draw close to God and learn His Word. Develop your own wonderful relationship with Him. Someone else's relationship to God is not primarily your responsibility; your own personal relationship with God is your responsibility. Get your eyes off others and focus on God.

Boaz was kind to Ruth. "And Boaz said unto her, At mealtime come thou hither, and eat of the bread, and dip thy morsel in the vinegar. And she sat beside the reapers: and he reached her parched corn, and she did eat, and was sufficed, and left" (vs. 14). We will compare Boaz's kindness to God's provision. God provides for our spiritual growth.

1. In his kindness to Ruth, Boaz offered for her to eat with the reapers at mealtime. We have already mentioned the servant who was over the reapers. In much the same way, God set a pastor over the rest of us. The reapers are like those in the ministry of the church who are workers, those who are serving in some capacity in the work of the ministry. The gleaners are those who are new to the Lord or those not saved. They come to church to get what they can get from the preacher's message, but they do not know much yet. All are welcome.

2. Notice also that food was available to her, but she herself had to go to get it. If you do not come to church, you will not hear the preacher's message from God's Word, and you will miss the fellowship and encouragement from others. You have to come.

3. All—the reapers and the gleaners—were invited to eat. The gleaners (those new to the Lord or perhaps yet unsaved) are just as welcome in the church as the reapers (the workers). All are invited and all are welcome.

4. She sat "beside" the reapers. She did not consider herself to be one of them. She was a gleaner; she was just getting what she could.

In a church, a gleaner may consider himself less of a Christian than one of the reapers. In my own experience, when I first started going to church, I looked around at the Christians and thought how I wanted to be like them; but I felt very incapable and very small. I felt privileged just to be able to sit among them and learn to know some of them. It is kind of foolish to feel that way, however. There is no separation between the reapers and the gleaners in a church service.

5. Boaz "reached her" parched corn. He gave her some on purpose. In a church service, the pastor extends an invitation at the end of the message for anyone to come to the Lord or to join the church family. Revelation 22:17 says, "And the Spirit and the bride say, Come. And let him that heareth say, Come. And let him that is athirst come. And whosoever will, let him take the water of life freely." The gift is available for everyone.

6. She ate as much as she needed, and she left. We do this every time we come to church. We listen to the pastor's message from God's Word, and we fellowship with other believers. It provides us a "booster shot" to give us encouragement to stay in God's Word and to love and obey Him. Then we go back out of the church, and we love and serve God and try to be a blessing to others.

> "So she gleaned in the field until even, and beat out that she had gleaned: and it was about an ephah of barley.
>
> "And she took it up, and went into the city: and her mother in law saw what she had gleaned: and

she brought forth, and gave to her that she had reserved after she was sufficed.

"And her mother in law said unto her, Where hast thou gleaned to day? and where wroughtest thou? blessed be he that did take knowledge of thee. And she shewed her mother in law with whom she had wrought, and said, The man's name with whom I wrought to day is Boaz.

"And Naomi said unto her daughter in law, Blessed be he of the Lord who hath not left off his kindness to the living and to the dead. And Naomi said unto her, The man is near of kin unto us, one of our next kinsmen."—Ruth 2:17–20.

After Ruth gleaned all day, she beat out what she had gleaned. That means that she laid out the stalks of grain and beat on them to separate the heads from the straw and the chaff from the grain. After that, the grain had to be winnowed. The grain was thrown into the air, and the wind caught the chaff and blew it away from the heavier grain, which fell back to the ground. When she was finished with that process, she ended up with an ephah of barley. An ephah was a little more than a bushel. A bushel of grain for one day's gleaning sounds like a great deal of grain and would be a lot for her to carry.

Ruth took it to Naomi and gave it to her. She also gave Naomi some food that she had kept from when she ate with the reapers. She "gave to her that she had reserved after she was sufficed."

Naomi was amazed. What a sweet young lady Ruth had been to her! How had she managed to accumulate so much grain, and where had she gotten this other food? Where had she been? Into whose field had she gone?

Naomi knew who Boaz was. He was a relative. How kind he had been to Ruth! This had been a great day. Ruth had gone out to do what she could do for Naomi. All she knew to do was to glean, gathering some food. God blessed her, taking her to Boaz's fields. She had worked hard. She had shown herself to be diligent and thankful for what she was allowed to do and to have.

The story does not end there. She continued to go out and glean. She did not wake up the next day and complain that she was worn out after working so hard. "So she kept fast by the maidens of Boaz to glean unto the end of barley harvest and of wheat harvest; and dwelt with her mother in law" (vs. 23).

Ruth served Naomi, and God provided for her. God uses people to give and provide for others who need it, but the blessings are coming from God. He is using His people to bless others. In the story of Ruth, Boaz made it his business to help Naomi and Ruth.

As you and I serve the Lord in working in the ministries of the church and in giving to others, as we love the Lord and learn His Word, He will provide for us in our spiritual growth as well as in material things. If we take care of God's business, He will take care of ours.

> "O taste and see that the Lord is good: blessed is the man that trusteth in him.

> "O fear the Lord, ye his saints: for there is no want to them that fear him.

> "The young lions do lack, and suffer hunger: but they that seek the Lord shall not want any good thing.

> "Come, ye children, hearken unto me: I will teach

you the fear of the Lord."—Ps. 34:8–11.

Psalm 34 was written by David when he was running for his life away from Saul. He still thought the Lord was good. He still thought that God provided all his need.

"There is no want" means that you will not need anything that you do not have. God will provide for you if you fear Him. Fear of the Lord is a good thing. "There is no want to them that fear him."

Ruth left all that she knew in order to seek the Lord. God made sure she was provided for.

He provides His Word to tell us what He wants us to know. He provides a local church ministry, a place where we can serve Him and where we have the fellowship of other believers to keep us on track. He provides a pastor who will teach us God's Word. We have to come to church in order to take advantage of all that God has provided for us.

Never be afraid to do all you can for the Lord. He will take care of you. Of course, that is not to say that you serve Him expecting something in return. Instead, the attitude is that you do not fret over your own needs, because if you are taking care of God's business, He will take care of yours.

Boaz Encouraging Ruth

"Beloved, let us love one another: for love is of God; and every one that loveth is born of God, and knoweth God."—I John 4:7.

In the previous chapter, we saw in the Book of Ruth, chapter 2, that Ruth had a servant's heart in doing whatever she could to help provide for herself and for Naomi. She worked hard doing what she knew to do, and God provided her needs. In this chapter of our study, we are again in Ruth 2, this time examining the way Boaz encouraged Ruth.

Boaz was a wealthy landowner, while Ruth was "only" a gleaner. In his station in life, Boaz was far superior to Ruth. She was "only" an alien from a heathen land. She was a widow and destitute, living with another destitute widow.

We have equated the reapers in the story with the workers, the servants in the ministry of the church. We equated the gleaners in the story with the visitors, those new to the Lord or perhaps unsaved. Boaz had given one servant responsibility over the other servants. This servant gives us a picture of the pastor in the ministry of the local church. Boaz gives us a very humble picture of God. He is the provider of the needs. He is the provider of the work to be done. He owns the land and fields that are part of the landscape of the Book of Ruth.

Boaz made it his business to encourage and help Ruth. We learned in Ruth 2:5–7 that Boaz had not met Ruth, but he had heard about her, and he was pleased with what he had heard.

Boaz Promised a *Place* for Ruth

Boaz encouraged Ruth to stay in his fields. "Then said Boaz unto Ruth, Hearest thou not, my daughter? Go not to glean in another field, neither go from hence, but abide here fast by my maidens" (vs. 8). It would have been simple for him to have said nothing to her and waited to see if she came back. It would have been just as simple for her to have gone to another field the next day. However, Boaz encouraged Ruth to stay in his field. He wanted to be the one to provide for her.

When new people come into our churches, we ought to be glad they are there. They may be well groomed and well dressed, or they may be dirty and smelly. They may be in between those two kinds of people. If they are still breathing, we want them in our church service, because we know that they will hear the Word of God there and they can grow closer to the Lord there, if they will just stay and open their hearts. We want them there because we know that our church people will encourage them, however they look.

When a new person comes into our church, we ought to encourage him or her like Boaz encouraged Ruth. He was helping to provide for her physical needs, but we can help provide for spiritual needs. We can tell folks how they can have a home in Heaven, if they are not already saved, and we can give the saved a place to serve God and grow closer to Him.

Some time ago a family came to the pastor and expressed interest in joining the church, but they were concerned that they would not be welcome. Their son was trying to get his life back together but had committed some things in the past for which he may have had to do jail time.

We wondered what that had to do with their joining the church. They said that because of their son's past, they were asked to leave the church they had previously been attending. They were amazed to think that they were welcome in our church. They said that their son was trying to turn his life around and do right but that even relatives watched and said, "Well, we'll see. If he gets things going well, then we'll welcome him"; but there was no intention of encouraging him. They were just going to wait and see.

If we are not going to encourage people like that, where will they find encouragement to draw closer to the Lord? We are so afraid of allowing a sinner into the church that we can't point anyone to the Lord. We forget that we are sinners too! We forget that it is only by the grace of God that we are not in the same situation!

Boaz encouraged Ruth to stay in his field. He would always make sure there was place for her, but he did not stop there.

Boaz Promised *Protection* for Ruth

Verse 9 says, "Let thine eyes be on the field that they do reap, and go thou after them: have I not charged the young men that they shall not touch thee?" Ruth knew that she would be allowed to work and would not have to worry about what the men might do to her. Boaz had instructed his men to leave her alone so she could work.

Boaz Promised *Provision* for Ruth

"When thou art athirst, go unto the vessels, and drink of that which the young men have drawn."

"And Boaz said unto her, At mealtime come thou hither, and eat of the bread, and dip thy morsel in the vinegar."—Ruth 2:9, 14.

Ruth was working in the heat and would need food and drink. Boaz said she could drink from the water that was already drawn from the well, and she was allowed to eat what he had provided for his own workers at mealtime.

Ruth Was Thankful

Verse 10 reveals Ruth's thankfulness: "Then she fell on her face, and bowed herself to the ground, and said unto him, Why have I found grace in thine eyes, that thou shouldest take knowledge of me, seeing I am a stranger?"

Ruth expected nothing from Boaz or anyone else. She knew that she was a stranger. She knew that people would look at her suspiciously. She was thankful for any kindness shown to her.

We can learn a valuable lesson from this as well. If we expect nothing from others, any kindness shown to us is cream on the top, and we will be thankful. If we expect others to do things for us, we will be disappointed because no matter how kind someone is, it will not be what we expected. Simply be thankful for every kindness.

May we be aware of this when people walk into our churches. Some new Christians are leaving their worldly friends. They may want to draw close to the Lord, and they see that they have to leave the lifestyle to which they have grown accustomed. It may be horrible, but it is all they know. What is it like to be a part of a church family? They have no idea. They are uncomfortable with their old friends because they know that they are not good for them. They are uncomfortable with their new church friends because they do not yet know them and they are not yet sure where they stand with them. They are not comfortable in either situation. We ought to encourage them.

We must love others and help them feel comfortable in the church family. They can learn to believe, trust, rest, be calm, and live holy and pure lives. They can learn the Bible and how to stand on God's Word sooner if they see us doing those things. We must encourage them to feel comfortable as part of the family of God. We must encourage all to focus on God.

> *"And Boaz answered and said unto her, It hath fully been shewed me, all that thou hast done unto thy mother in law since the death of thine husband: and how thou hast left thy father and thy mother, and the land of thy nativity, and art come unto a people which thou knewest not heretofore.*
>
> *"The Lord recompense thy work, and a full reward be given thee of the Lord God of Israel, under whose wings thou art come to trust."*—Vss. 11, 12.

Boaz realized what an upheaval it was in Ruth's life to leave her home and all that she knew. She left her family and friends. She left the worship of the false god,

Chemosh. She had never known anything else; but when she learned about the one true God, she left all she knew to follow Him. Boaz was very impressed with that. He understood that she was trusting God and that doing so was all new to her.

"Then she said, Let me find favour in thy sight, my lord; for that thou hast comforted me, and for that thou hast spoken friendly unto thine handmaid, though I be not like unto one of thine handmaidens" (vs. 13). Boaz had already shown kindness to Ruth. She had already received blessings because of her willingness to follow God, as well as her sweet servant's spirit. Yet in this verse she requests, "Let me find favour in thy sight." What is going on here?

Ruth recognized that Boaz owed her nothing but he had been very gracious, kind and welcoming to her. She was thankful for every kindness extended to her. Without the kindness that Boaz had extended, she would have had nothing; that was why she was out gleaning in his fields. In addition, without the continued kindness of someone like Boaz, Ruth and Naomi may have starved. She asked for continued kindness. This was another indication that she was thankful for what had been provided for her.

Think of your own life. Think of the many blessings that God has given you. Where would you be without them?

This has become very apparent to me in recent times. I know that God has greatly blessed me; He has given me far more than I deserve. He has allowed me to have a Christian husband and a Christian home. He has allowed me to have friends who love God and His

Word. He has allowed me to learn His Word.

Recently I have asked God to continue to bless me because I am afraid of what my life would be like without the blessings of God. The first couple times I prayed that way, I felt like I was being selfish; but I do not believe that it is selfish. Instead, I believe that it is more that I'm realizing I have nothing and am nothing without God's blessings. I know what my life was like before I got saved, and I am very thankful for where He has brought me. I am thankful that I do not have to go back there. I want God to continue to bless me.

Be thankful for what God has given you and ask Him for continued blessings.

> *"And when she was risen up to glean, Boaz commanded his young men, saying, Let her glean even among the sheaves, and reproach her not:*
>
> *"And let fall also some of the handfuls of purpose for her, and leave them, that she may glean them, and rebuke her not."*—Vss. 15,16.

Boaz commanded his reapers to make sure there was plenty for her to pick up. He told them to let some extra fall as they were reaping and even to let her pick up from the sheaves. The sheaves are the bundles that the reapers had already gathered! Boaz was surely helping Ruth to have plenty to take to Naomi.

This was another instance of Boaz's encouraging Ruth. He was enhancing her success, but she still had to glean. She still had to pick it up, beat it out, thresh and winnow, then carry it home; but Boaz supported her efforts.

Ruth accepted every kindness from Boaz. She knew that

without it she had nothing. At every step, she was thankful and continued to work diligently and unassumingly.

Some new Christians will come to church and be all excited about what they see; but when they see the Lord start to work in their lives, they get scared because it is all unfamiliar to them. They back away and stop coming to church so much, and we lose them. If we do not continue to encourage those folks who really need our encouragement, we will lose our influence on them to keep their focus on the Lord.

We must make sure we do what Boaz did. He gave Ruth a place to glean, and he gave her protection and provision. He encouraged her success by instructing his reapers to leave some extra for her and by allowing her to glean even among the sheaves. He wanted to be sure she was provided for.

Let's encourage our "gleaners," welcome them, tell them we are glad they are in our church. Invite them to our Sunday school classes. Love them, helping them feel comfortable in the church family where God can bless them.

When we first went to our church, there was a couple who had already left before we got there. They just wanted out. One of the men told my husband about them. He and my husband went to visit the couple. They had a very pleasant visit with them; and after they were there for a while, the man warmed up and sounded like he might decide to visit again. His wife, however, was friendly only as long as they were having general conversation. As soon as there was any mention of coming back to church, she threw up a wall and did not want to talk about it.

The next Sunday the husband of that couple was in church while his wife was at work. "Your wife doesn't know you are here, does she?" my husband asked.

"No! But I just didn't want to stay away," he said.

We were excited that he had come, but that evening I was sitting on the platform for orchestra, and he and she both came in! I was so excited that she had come. After the service, I ran to the back of the auditorium and reached out to shake her hand. I drew her close to me and said, "I know you didn't want to come, but I am just glad you're here"; and I gave her a hug.

They have been in our church ever since then. I didn't think much about it, but several months later, that man was talking to my husband. Something was said about the fact that they had left and that we were so glad they decided to come back after we came.

"I'll tell you what really did it for my wife," the man told us. "She had not wanted to come back, but your wife came to her the first week we were back and told her that she was glad she was here and gave her a hug."

I was amazed to know that such a small thing meant that much to her. You will never know what small kindnesses can do for someone. Those people were hurting. I did not even know that I was doing anything for her; I was just glad she had come.

We don't know what kind of hurt may be in the hearts of people who walk through the doors of our churches. There is a reason they have decided to leave the church where they have been, or there is a reason they have decided to come to church even though they have not been going to any other church. They need to be encouraged. They need to be loved.

Boaz did whatever he could to encourage Ruth. Let's encourage others. Let's love others.

Ruth's Request

"I am Ruth thine handmaid: spread therefore thy skirt over thine handmaid; for thou art a near kinsman."—Ruth 3:9.

We have seen what a blessing Boaz was to Ruth as he encouraged her in her efforts to sustain herself and Naomi. It would seem that she should have been of no consequence to him, and yet he paid special attention to her, even on the very first day that she was gleaning in his field. He made sure she had plenty of grain to gather and to take home for Naomi. However, she still had to do the work. After the first day that Ruth gleaned, she took home so much grain that Naomi wondered where she had been. When Ruth said that she had been in Boaz's field, Naomi was very excited. She knew that Boaz was a close relative to her husband's family.

We learned in Ruth 2:23 that Ruth stayed in Boaz's fields through barley harvest and through wheat harvest. Harvesting of each of those grains would have lasted about a month. So if Ruth continued to glean in Boaz's field all during that time, he had plenty of opportunity to watch her and see the depth of her character.

Now we are going to look in Ruth 3 at an event that

is foreign to us but which continues to present the sweetness of Ruth and the kindness of Boaz.

The chapter begins, "Then Naomi her mother in law said unto her, My daughter, shall I not seek rest for thee, that it may be well with thee?" (vs. 1). The rest to which Naomi refers in this verse is the rest in marriage. When people are wed, their marriage ought to be a place of rest for them. When a man and woman meet at the marriage altar, they should promise each other "until death do us part." They make that promise public "before God and these witnesses." The concern of finding the right match is over. A husband and wife ought to be comfortable with each other so that there is no more wondering where each stands with the other. There is no more thought of trying to capture the other's attention, no more wondering what each thinks of the other. The attention, then, ought to be focused on loving and giving to the other spouse.

That is how it ought to be. In my own experience, I remember noticing that feeling of rest and calm after I got married. I remember thinking that I would not have to date anymore and wonder if a certain person would be right for me. I remember thinking how wonderful it was. It breaks my heart to hear people complain about their spouses.

Years ago I had a high-school clarinet student whose mother and father had moved to this country from India. One day this girl's father was talking to my husband during her lesson, and he learned some interesting things about this man. He said that he did not understand American couples and how mates are always fighting with each other and how many get divorced. He believed that marriage partners have to decide to get along with each other. He lived in a place where the marriages were arranged. He met his wife fifteen minutes before they were married!

In this country, you actually get to pick your own spouse. How, then, can you spend your life fighting with each other?

I know personally a man and woman who have been married for fifty years and have a beautiful, loving relationship. He says that when they first got married, they fought like cats and dogs for about two weeks. He decided he could not live like that and that they needed to figure out how they could get along with each other. They talked and determined that they were not going to fight. They determined that they would enjoy each other. It was just a matter of making a decision.

Several years after we were married, my husband told me that he had decided long before he got married that he was not going to fight with his wife. You must realize that when you fight with your husband, you are teaching your children that this is the way to deal with differences in relationships. I have had to learn not to lash out at things. A person can learn to respond calmly to things he does not like. How did I learn that? My husband had decided he would not fight. I learned it from him.

It takes two people to fight. If one of the parties does not show up for the fight, it does not take place! You cannot control what your husband does, but you can control what you do. Even if he lashes out at you, if you do not lash back, there is no fight.

Remember Proverbs 15:1, which says, "A soft answer turneth away wrath." If wrath comes at you but you respond with a soft answer, you completely diffuse the wrath, so there is no fight. When my own children fought when they were small, I could always hear, "He started it!" My answer to that was always "It doesn't matter who started it; you both kept it going. It takes two people to fight."

Proverbs 18:22 says, "Whoso findeth a wife findeth a good thing, and obtaineth favour of the LORD." Make sure your husband found a good thing when he found you. Enjoy your husband. Work at *building* your relationship instead of knocking it down. You picked your husband, so there must have been something about him that you thought was wonderful! Encourage him in everything that is good about him.

My husband and I make an effort to encourage each other. If you do not do that, the Bible says that you are foolish. "Every wise woman buildeth her house: but the foolish plucketh it down with her hands" (14:1). If you do not perpetuate a loving relationship with your husband and if there is fighting going on, you are plucking down your house; but if you are wise, you will build it. You can decide to have a wonderful relationship.

It appears that Naomi had no intention of marrying again, but she was not holding Ruth to that. Ruth was much younger, and it would have been prudent for her to marry again. We saw that if a man died, having had no children, then his brother was obligated to marry his widow. The firstborn child would be named after the deceased brother, perpetuating his name (Deut. 25:5, 6).

That requirement applied only to brothers, but it appears that the people of Israel expanded that law of God to a custom in which the next-nearest relative could fulfill the same responsibility. Naomi knew from the first day that Ruth went to glean in the fields that Boaz was a near relative; and apparently, as far as she knew, he was her nearest relative. She had also seen the extensive kindness that he had shown to Ruth. She suggested something to Ruth that seems very strange to us.

> *"And now is not Boaz of our kindred, with whose maidens thou wast? Behold, he winnoweth barley to night in the threshingfloor.*
>
> *"Wash thyself therefore, and anoint thee, and put thy raiment upon thee, and get thee down to the floor: but make not thyself known unto the man, until he shall have done eating and drinking.*
>
> *"And it shall be, when he lieth down, that thou shalt mark the place where he shall lie, and thou shalt go in, and uncover his feet, and lay thee down; and he will tell thee what thou shalt do."*— Ruth 3:2–4.

Naomi was basically suggesting that Ruth ask Boaz to marry her because he was a close relative. Although this sounds very strange to us, we must remember the difference in culture caused people to think of things differently than we do. Naomi instructed Ruth to get cleaned up and dressed up nicely and make sure she smelled really nice, because she was going to meet Boaz.

Let's look at the situation first. Boaz was winnowing barley in the threshing floor. The threshing floor was a flat area, stone or concrete, where the grain on the stalks was laid in a pile. An ox would be used to pull a heavy pallet across the grain, crushing the stalk and breaking it from the head of grain. The farmer might stand on the pallet to make it heavier. The ox would walk around and around the threshing floor, breaking the heads from the stalks and the grain from the chaff.

After this process, the grain was thrown into the air. The heavier grain fell back down onto a pile. The straw, the stalk of the grain, was blown away to a pile nearby because it had a little bit of weight. The chaff blew away in the wind and scattered.

Although this was hard work, it became the custom to make it into a feast time in celebration of the harvesting of the crop and the provision of food that the crop was to them. (The men did the same thing when they had a sheepshearing.) That is why Naomi instructed Ruth to wait until Boaz had finished eating and drinking. The custom of that day allowed the workers to work late on their grain. If it was too late to return to their homes, they simply slept at the threshing floor with their grain. Then they would be ready to begin working again early the next morning.

In addition, in order to ensure that their grain would not be stolen from the threshing floor during the night, the men slept there next to their grain. So the men worked hard all day, had a party, and then slept right there. Boaz would not be the only one at the threshing floor that night, and the workers did not expect any women to be there.

The obvious question arises here as to why Ruth did not approach Boaz to make this request when she was gleaning in his field day after day. Perhaps it was because this was a rather delicate topic of discussion, and if she followed Naomi's instructions, Ruth would have a quiet, private audience with Boaz, away from his servants.

> *"And she said unto her, All that thou sayest unto me I will do.*
>
> *"And she went down unto the floor, and did accord-*

ing to all that her mother in law bade her.

"And when Boaz had eaten and drunk, and his heart was merry, he went to lie down at the end of the heap of corn: and she came softly, and uncovered his feet, and laid her down."—Vss. 5–7.

Apparently it was dark. He had a large blanket with which to cover himself. Apparently she waited until he had fallen asleep. Ruth picked up the end of the blanket and lay there at his feet. Then she simply waited.

"And it came to pass at midnight, that the man was afraid, and turned himself: and, behold, a woman lay at his feet.

"And he said, Who art thou? And she answered, I am Ruth thine handmaid: spread therefore thy skirt over thine handmaid; for thou art a near kinsman."—Vss. 8, 9.

When Boaz awoke, he was afraid because he realized there was a woman there. It was very dark, and Boaz had to ask who she was. Ruth identified herself as his "handmaid." She was going to ask him to marry her as the nearest relative of her deceased husband, but she still called herself a servant to Boaz. After identifying herself, Ruth simply asked that he spread his skirt over her. Ruth had made her request, and that was all she said.

What did this mean? When Ruth asked Boaz to spread his skirt over her, she was asking him to provide protection and support for her. Because he was a near kinsman, she was asking him to marry her; and he also knew that this meant that their firstborn child would carry the name of her deceased husband. What would Boaz say? Would he be willing to take the responsibility of the kinsman?

"And he said, Blessed be thou of the LORD, *my daughter: for thou hast shewed more kindness in the latter end than at the beginning, inasmuch as thou followedst not young men, whether poor or rich.*

"And now, my daughter, fear not; I will do to thee all that thou requirest: for all the city of my people doth know that thou art a virtuous woman."—Vss. 10, 11.

Boaz was pleased to do as Ruth had asked him.

There are several things to notice in these verses about how he responded to her. He called her his "daughter." It appears that probably Boaz was a well-established man, likely significantly older than Ruth. He knew that she had left her family and had moved to Bethlehem with her mother-in-law after her husband's death. He was impressed with her. He pronounced a blessing on her because of what she had done.

By her asking Boaz to do the part of a kinsman and marry her, Ruth showed that she was not looking for a man who suited her own desires, but that she was concerned with following the spirit of the Law of God in marrying her deceased husband's relative, thus perpetuating his family name. It was not sinful lust or personal desires that had taken her to that threshing floor that night.

Boaz said, "Fear not." He was basically telling her not to worry about a thing. He would take care of the entire situation. He said he would do as she had asked. What a comfort it must have been to Ruth! She had to have been apprehensive about this meeting. It was all so strange. She waited until he was finished eating and drinking and then waited until he went to sleep, after which she lay at his feet until he awoke and noticed that she was there. No wonder he said, "Fear not!" Boaz continued to be caring, loving and tender toward Ruth.

As we read the Book of Ruth, we see that at every turn in the road, Ruth did the right thing. That is why Boaz said in verse 11 that "all the city of my people doth know that thou art a virtuous woman." In the next chapter we will discuss how everyone could have known that Ruth was a virtuous woman.

There was one other consideration, however, before Boaz could agree to marry Ruth.

> *"And now it is true that I am thy near kinsman: howbeit there is a kinsman nearer than I.*
>
> *"Tarry this night, and it shall be in the morning, that if he will perform unto thee the part of a kinsman, well; let him do that kinsman's part: but if he will not do the part of a kinsman to thee, then will I do the part of a kinsman to thee, as the LORD liveth: lie down until the morning."—Vss. 12, 13.*

Ruth would have to wait until Boaz contacted another kinsman who was more closely related than he was. Ruth might not be able to marry Boaz after all. She had grown to know him through the kindnesses that he had shown to her.

It appears in these verses that Ruth did not know the other relative to whom Boaz referred, since he did not mention his name; but she could be assured that someone would take her in so that she would not have to be a widow anymore. Boaz assured her that if the other relative did not take her, then he would do it. Ruth could leave the threshing floor knowing that she would have a husband, but she did not know for sure who it would be.

> "Also he said, Bring the vail that thou hast upon thee, and hold it. And when she held it, he measured six measures of barley, and laid it on her: and she went into the city.
>
> "And when she came to her mother in law, she said, Who art thou, my daughter? And she told her all that the man had done to her.
>
> "And she said, These six measures of barley gave he me; for he said to me, Go not empty unto thy mother in law.
>
> "Then said she, Sit still, my daughter, until thou know how the matter will fall: for the man will not be in rest, until he have finished the thing this day."— Vss. 15–18.

It seems strange that Naomi would ask, "Who art thou, my daughter?" After all, she certainly knew who Ruth was. The question was, "Well, are you a bride? Did Boaz agree to marry you?" Naomi was asking how the meeting went.

Before Ruth had left the threshing floor, Boaz had made another very kind gesture toward her. Prior to this time, he had made sure that she had plenty of grain to pick up so that she would have enough to take to Naomi, though she still had to do all the work. However, on this occasion he gave her grain that was already gathered, threshed and winnowed.

Six measures of grain would be six omers. Ten omers would make an ephah. An ephah was a little more than a bushel, so six measures of grain would have been a little more than half a bushel. She had not gone to the threshing floor dressed for work; therefore, she would probably not have been able to carry as much as she did when she went out to glean. It is probable that Boaz gave

Ruth as much grain as she could carry. This was another kindness to Ruth and Naomi.

Ruth left there with the promise that either Boaz or the other relative, who was closer, would marry her. She and Naomi would no longer have to be without support and protection. They would have to wait until Boaz met with the other man before they would know who Ruth's husband would be, but Naomi felt certain that Boaz would deal with the matter very soon.

What a relief this was to Naomi and Ruth! They certainly waited with great anticipation. It seems obvious that they would hope that Boaz would marry Ruth. After all, she had certainly grown to have great respect for him.

Although this entire event seems very strange to us, it remains a very sweet, warm story. Ruth had shown herself to be a very special person, and Boaz had shown himself to be a very caring person.

The more we study Ruth and Boaz, the more special they seem to become. Let us continue to recognize their positive qualities and allow them to teach us how we ought to trust God and how we ought to treat others.

Ruth, the Virtuous Woman

"All the city of my people doth know that thou art a virtuous woman."—Ruth 3:11.

In the previous chapter we found that Ruth went at night to the threshing floor where she could have a quiet, personal conversation with Boaz. She asked him to fulfill the part of the near kinsman, which would mean that he would marry her and their firstborn child would carry the name of her deceased husband, Mahlon. Boaz told Ruth that there was another kinsman who was nearer than he. To find out who her husband was going to be, Ruth would have to wait until Boaz talked with the nearer kinsman about the matter. Boaz agreed to marry Ruth if the nearer kinsman did not.

Now we look in more detail at Boaz's response in Ruth 3:11, where he told Ruth that everyone knew she was a virtuous woman. There are several things in this passage that show again what a very unusual person Ruth was.

First, let's define what it means to be virtuous. What was Boaz actually saying to Ruth?

I did a little word search on this word "virtuous." My findings were not what I expected, and I was very encouraged by what I learned. It is used only three times in the Bible.

1. It is found in this passage in Ruth.

2. It is found in Proverbs 31:10: "Who can find a virtuous woman? for her price is far above rubies."

3. It is found in Proverbs 12:4: "A virtuous woman is a crown to her husband."

Then, in adverb form, in Proverbs 31:29, a woman is said to have done "virtuously."

The original word means "a force, whether of men, means or other resources." Interestingly, those three times that it is found in the Bible, it refers to a **woman.** If it is a force of men, means or other resources, then it is a strength or a power. A virtuous woman is a strong woman.

While it is true that the English word "virtuous" is used only three times in the Bible, the Hebrew word that is translated "virtuous" is also translated into several other English words. Look at these words: *able; activity* (like "men of activity," that is, men with capabilities or talents that are useful in the building of the tabernacle or the temple, for example); *band of men* (soldiers); *company* (army); *forces; host* (the army of a nation); *might; power; riches; strength* (these verses all referred to God's strength); *strong;* and *substance.*

I did not look up every single reference where this Hebrew word was found, but I looked up a lot of them; and every one that I read referred to **men,** or as in the case of the word "strength," the word was used in reference to God. Always the word had the connotation of strength or power. When referring to a **woman,** the word was "virtuous."

It is also interesting to me that the word "virtue" is used in the New Testament. Three times it is used of virtue coming from Jesus. In Mark 5:25–34, there was a woman who had been bleeding for twelve years. She had spent everything she had going to doctors who could do nothing to heal her. When she saw Jesus in a large crowd, she thought that she could be healed if she could only touch the hem of His robe. When she touched Jesus' robe, she was healed. Jesus could tell that "virtue had gone out of him" (vs. 30). What is the virtue there? It was miraculous power—the power of God to heal.

There is another word translated "virtue" in the New Testament.

> *"Finally, brethren, whatsoever things are true, whatsoever things are honest, whatsoever things are just, whatsoever things are pure, whatsoever things are lovely, whatsoever things are of good report; if there be any virtue, and if there be any praise, think on these things."*—Phil. 4:8.

> *"And beside this, giving all diligence, add to your faith virtue; and to virtue knowledge."*—II Pet. 1:5.

The word in these passages means "manliness, valor, excellence."

So I must conclude that when God wanted to show a virtuous woman, she would be a strong woman, a good woman. Let's look at Proverbs 31:10: "Who can find a virtuous woman? for her price is far above rubies."

The question seems to be rhetorical, does it not? The way the question is presented makes it appear that the obvious answer is that nobody can find one. Her price is far above rubies. The ruby is hard, second only to the diamond in hardness, and very valuable. The value of the virtuous woman and the value of wisdom are both compared to the value of the ruby.

> *"She* [wisdom] *is more precious than rubies: and all the things thou canst desire are not to be compared unto her."*

> *"For wisdom is better than rubies; and all the things that may be desired are not to be compared to it* [wisdom]."—Prov. 3:15; 8:11.

Wisdom cannot be compared to anything else that you can desire, and it is better than rubies. In Proverbs 31:10, the price of a virtuous woman is "far above rubies." Now I would say that I would like to be one of those virtuous women, but this verse says that such a woman is not to be found, and she is much more valuable than rubies. We realize that the woman in Proverbs 31 is not a living, particular woman but is the picture of what a virtuous woman would look like if one could be found.

It is interesting to notice, then, that in all of the Bible, Ruth is the only real woman who is called virtuous. How special that is! She is in a league all by herself.

Boaz certainly paid Ruth a high compliment. You will notice that he said everyone knew she was a virtuous woman. There is an obvious question to ask: How did everyone know that Ruth was a virtuous woman?

Ruth arrived in Bethlehem at the beginning of barley harvest, and she had been gleaning in his fields for about two months. No one knew her when she arrived, and it appears that she simply did what she needed to do. She remained unassuming, apparently soft-spoken, diligent, and responsible. She had obviously been very kind to her mother-in-law. They were living in the city, so she had certainly come to know some of the young ladies by this time.

What had people learned about her? First of all, they

were able to see her kindness to Naomi. Second, some people were able to watch her work. The servant that was set over the reapers told Boaz the very first day that she had worked hard except for only a small break. They saw her go to the fields to glean, day after day. The text tells us that she kept working through the weeks of harvest. "So she kept fast by the maidens of Boaz to glean unto the end of barley harvest and of wheat harvest; and dwelt with her mother in law" (Ruth 2:23).

There is a lot of activity in that one little verse. There are two months of living going on there. The people in Bethlehem lived and worked and played and ate and did housework and more for two months. None of that is recorded in the Bible for us. They had some time to witness Ruth's character during that time. They learned to know her, at least to some degree. After learning to know her, everybody realized that she was a good person.

Boaz agreed that he would do all that Ruth needed (which was to marry her), for everyone knew that she was a virtuous woman (3:11). The emphasis here is on the word "for." She was reaping the benefits of doing right. It appears that Boaz was more than willing, maybe even honored, to do as Ruth had asked because it was obvious to everyone that she was good and virtuous.

She had developed in that place a good name. According to Proverbs 22:1, "A good name is rather to be chosen than great riches, and loving favour rather than silver and gold."

It was because of Ruth's good name that Boaz was willing to agree to do what she had asked. A good name has many benefits. It is more valuable to a person than great riches. It was because of her good name, as well as Boaz's good name, that we read in Ruth 3:14, "And she lay at his feet until the morning: and she rose up before one could know another. And he said, Let it not be known that a woman came into the floor."

This means that Ruth stayed until morning but left before it was light enough to be able to recognize anyone. Her eyes had grown accustomed to the dark, and she could see just enough to walk home, but visibility was not yet good enough for people to recognize one another. Why would Ruth stay till morning?

1. It was not safe for her to walk home alone during the night. She waited until the sun had just started to come up.

2. She was leaving before anyone else could know that she had been there.

This too has to do with her good name. Boaz said, "Let it not be known that a woman came into the floor." Ruth had been with Boaz all night, but they had not done anything inappropriate. However, if people thought that she had been with Boaz all night, they might very well have thought that something was amiss and might have started to talk. Ruth had shown herself to be virtuous and honorable. She had developed a positive reputation. Really, her virtue, her goodness, was all she had. People thought very highly of Ruth.

If people had started talking about the fact that Ruth was with Boaz at the threshing floor all night, good people would have been disturbed by it and disappointed in her. It would have troubled them to think that she might not be what they had thought she was. Others, of the not-so-good variety, would have been pleased to have discovered some "dirt" on her. They would have concluded, "See, she's not all she appears to be!" Then they would have thought that maybe *they* didn't look so bad.

So Ruth stayed all night for the sake of safety; then she left early before anyone could know that she had been there, for the sake of her testimony.

This is very important. Do people know that they can trust you to do right? Can people trust you with their children? Can people trust you to conduct yourself in a Christlike way? Can people trust you to pay them and pay them on time? Can people count on you to do what you say you will do? Can people trust you if they loan something to you? Will you return it as you promised, when you promised, and in good shape? Can people ask you to do something and know that you will pay attention to whatever details are required to do a good job? Do you have a good name?

Maintaining your good name is just as important as developing it in the first place. Even though people have been able to trust you concerning all the things just mentioned, as soon as you violate any one of those things in someone's eyes, your testimony is seriously marred. It will take a long time to regain a good name after you have lost it. It is much simpler to develop a good name in the first place than it is to regain it. Be sure to maintain your good name. Keep your testimony pure.

Boaz told Ruth that everybody knew she was a virtuous woman. She had gone to the threshing floor that night for very honorable reasons, and she and Boaz had done nothing inappropriate. People thought very highly of Ruth. What if people learned that she had been at the threshing floor that night? They would no longer think that she was a virtuous woman.

This is where the truth of I Thessalonians 5:22 applies:

"Abstain from all appearance of evil."

Yes, avoid evil. Do not do wrong. It is not right to do wrong. It is important not only to avoid sin but also to avoid scandal. If someone *says* you did something wrong, there is scandal. So if you just *look* like you may have done something wrong, then you are setting yourself up for the destruction of your testimony. You need to remain above reproach.

I have a question: Why would Ruth do this? Why would she go to the threshing floor that night where there was a party for men and no women were expected? Why would she lift Boaz's blanket and lie at his feet, frightening him in the middle of the night? Why would she put herself in a position where she had to leave early in the morning before the sun was fully up so that no one would know that she had been there? Why did she do something about which she had to be sneaky in order to avoid scandal?

It appears that *if* there is fault to be placed for her actions, it should lie on Naomi. After all, Ruth was obeying her mother-in-law. It seems she was right to do so. Naomi was familiar with local customs and practices; and since she told Ruth to do such a thing, then surely it must have been acceptable. Would she have wanted to dirty her own daughter-in-law's purity? It would not seem so.

Still, it seems it could have been fuel for scandal. It appears that Boaz did not rebuke Ruth for doing something that was unbecoming to her. As a matter of fact, he praised her for wanting to obey the spirit of God's commands (in raising up seed for the name of her deceased husband) instead of looking for a husband that suited her desires. It also appears that he recognized her apprehension when he said, "Fear not."

Boaz had told Ruth that there was a kinsman nearer than he was and that he would have to be consulted in this matter. However, Boaz promised her that he would marry her if the other relative did not.

This brings us to one other consideration. Boaz told Ruth in verse 11 to "fear not." She had presented her request to Boaz, and she did not have to think about it anymore. He would take possession of the concern, and he would see to the settling of it.

There is a lesson here for us as well. I realize that Ruth turned her concern over to Boaz, but we can apply this to our own lives in the need for us to turn our problems over to God.

First Peter 5:7 says, "Casting all your care upon him; for he careth for you." Turn over your problems to God. He loves you. He cares about you. He wants to take care of your needs. Another Scripture says, "Cast thy burden upon the LORD, and he shall sustain thee: he shall never suffer the righteous to be moved" (Ps. 55:22). Turn your problems over to God. He will take care of them, and He will hold you up.

We talked about this verse before: "Commit thy way unto the LORD; trust also in him; and he shall bring it to pass" (37:5). Turn your life over to God and trust Him. If you obey Him, He will make sure you do what He has planned for you to do.

If you take a problem or a concern to the Lord and ask Him to take care of it, leave it with Him and forget about it. Trust Him and continue to do what you are supposed to do. He may not resolve your concern the way you would have, but you turned it over to Him. Always remember that God is much wiser than you are. Whatever He works in your life, trust Him believing that He did what was best. It may not be what you would have chosen, but are you trusting God or not?

A friend of mine came to me one day and said that something had happened at church, but it was just a family matter. It had nothing to do with church; it just happened to be there. It had nothing to do with her; it just happened to concern part of her family. Someone did something to another. One of the parties went to the other to try to make things right, but the other party was making no effort to resolve the situation. The whole thing upset her, even though she had nothing to do with it. She said that she had prayed and prayed over it. She had prayed every day. She had tried to turn it over to the Lord, but it still upset her, and she could not stop thinking about it. She asked me what she should do.

"Stop praying about it," I told her.

"What?" she said. It seemed like a strange thing for me to say.

"Pray about it, turn it over to God, then let go of it, and let Him take care of it. If you continue to bring it up to yourself day after day, you will never forget it, and you will continue to stew over it, and there is no benefit in stewing over it. After all, you already said that it really has nothing to do with you. Give it to God and let it go."

God knows what to do even when you do not. Give the problem to Him and get it off your desk!

One word of warning is in order here, however. If you have made a mess out of your life with bad choices, even though you may ask God to fix it all back up, He will not take away the natural consequences of your actions. Don't think you can live like the Devil and then expect God to clean up the mess. You got yourself into the mess by your actions, even though you knew better. If you smoke for sixty years and develop lung problems, it is unreasonable to ask God for healing for your lungs when in fact you caused the problem yourself. If you spend all your money on cigarettes and gambling and dig yourself into a big financial hole, it is unreasonable to pray to God to fix your financial troubles. He already gave you the necessary resources, but you "spent your lunch money on bubble gum." God will not remove the natural consequences of your actions.

I am also not talking about things to which you yourself need to tend. If you have not been paying your taxes and you receive notice from the IRS that you owe them a large sum of back taxes, that is not the time to pray and let it go. You have to respond to the IRS. Self-inflicted problems are not going to go away just because you pray and ask for relief.

However, when you are doing right and living right and a problem comes your way that you do not know how to handle, give it to God and let Him deal with it.

We learn, then, that Ruth had developed a radiant testimony of being a virtuous woman and that Boaz tried to help her maintain her reputation. We also learn that once she turned over to Boaz the possession of the matter under consideration, she stepped back and waited. She cast her care on the shoulders of Boaz, who promised her that he would deal with the matter and she need not fear.

We can apply that principle to ourselves. Once we give our problems to God, we can leave them with Him. He will deal with them.

The Transaction

"Ruth the Moabitess, the wife of Mahlon, have I purchased to be my wife, to raise up the name of the dead upon his inheritance."—Ruth 4:10.

We have looked at the events in Ruth 3, when Ruth went to the threshing floor to ask Boaz to take her in marriage. He knew that meant that their firstborn child would carry the name of her deceased husband. We saw that Boaz told Ruth that everyone knew she was a virtuous woman. We discussed the importance of maintaining a good testimony.

Here we look at the events of the following day. Boaz wasted no time attending to the matter at hand.

> *"Then went Boaz up to the gate, and sat him down there: and, behold, the kinsman of whom Boaz spake came by; unto whom he said, Ho, such a one! turn aside, sit down here. And he turned aside, and sat down.*
>
> *"And he took ten men of the elders of the city, and said, Sit ye down here. And they sat down."*—Ruth 4:1, 2.

Let's look at the gate at which Boaz sat. A city in those days was a space with houses and streets, surrounded by walls which were a defense against intruders.

Surrounding the city were the farms and fields of grain to which Ruth had gone to glean.

The walls of the city might have been high, wide, strong, and complete with soldiers standing guard. There may have been one, sometimes two, gates in a city. The gate was obviously to allow people to go in and out of the city. The facts that the gate was where the people went in and out and that it had to be moveable to allow passage made the gate the weakest part of the city wall. As cities were built, the gates became larger, thicker, stronger, more fortified, and more complex in an effort to increase security.

It appears obvious as well that almost everyone in the city would pass through the gate during the course of the day. This may be why the gate became such an important part of the life of the city. It became something more than a gate for passage. It became a marketplace. People in the city set up shop there, and people from other cities would set up outside the gate, selling their wares.

It became the seat of government as well. People paid their taxes there, and legal matters were settled there— like in a courthouse. The gate was also the place to hold meetings of various kinds.

That is why Boaz went to the gate and sat there. The other kinsman of whom he spake would go by there at some time that day. Perhaps Boaz went early in the morning so that he would surely see the man before he went to his place of work.

Boaz called to the man and asked him to sit down. Then he called for ten other men to sit down. They were elders of the city. Did they just happen to be

there? Possibly it was their job to be at the gate to trans-
act any business proceedings that would go on that day.
It does not appear that Boaz had an appointment with
anyone. It seems that he approached the gate and this
whole matter as one having authority in the city. He
asked the men to witness the transaction that was about
to take place.

It does not appear that Boaz asked any one of them
his opinion about the transaction, but it seems they were
present merely to serve as witnesses. This may not have
always been the case. Perhaps there were times when
those men acted as judges on a particular matter, but in
this case Boaz needed only witnesses.

A man who sat at the gate was an important man to
the city. Actually, it is very likely that Boaz was one of
the elders of the city. After all, he was a mighty man of
wealth.

After seating the witnesses, Boaz turned his attention
to his kinsman.

> *"And he said unto the kinsman, Naomi, that is
> come again out of the country of Moab, selleth a par-
> cel of land, which was our brother Elimelech's:*
>
> *"And I thought to advertise thee, saying, Buy it
> before the inhabitants, and before the elders of my
> people. If thou wilt redeem it, redeem it: but if thou
> wilt not redeem it, then tell me, that I may know: for
> there is none to redeem it beside thee; and I am after
> thee. And he said, I will redeem it."*—Vss. 3, 4.

Notice that Boaz had mentioned nothing of Ruth in
these verses. He offered his kinsman the privilege to purchase the land which had belonged to Elimelech. Perhaps the land had been mortgaged when they left in the

famine, and Naomi did not have the resources to buy
back the equity of it. In any case, a kinsman could purchase the land, thus keeping it in the family. The kinsman agreed to redeem the land. Surely this would be a
welcome addition to his own land holdings.

> *"Then said Boaz, What day thou buyest the field
> of the hand of Naomi, thou must buy it also of Ruth
> the Moabitess, the wife of the dead, to raise up the
> name of the dead upon his inheritance.*
>
> *"And the kinsman said, I cannot redeem it for
> myself, lest I mar mine own inheritance: redeem thou
> my right to thyself; for I cannot redeem it."*—Vss. 5, 6.

After the kinsman agreed to accept the *privilege* of
taking possession of the land, then Boaz presented the
duty of marrying Ruth and raising up seed to Mahlon.
The kinsman was not willing to take that responsibility.
Perhaps he was already married. Perhaps he was unwill-
ing to share his estate with another family. (Any first
child born to Ruth would go to Mahlon's name instead
of to the near kinsman's. Other children born to Ruth
might expect part of the near kinsman's estate, and this
man was not willing to make that commitment.) In any
case, he felt it unwise to accept this responsibility.

It appears that the kinsman did not know Ruth as
Boaz had learned to know her. Boaz knew her to be virtuous, diligent, responsible, kind, and loving. The pic-
tures we see of Ruth portray her as a beautiful young
lady, although we really have no reason to think that she
was. After all, the months of working in the hot sun, as
well as the beating, threshing and winnowing of grain,
would have made her sun-baked and worn. However,
her inner beauty was not diminished by her outward
appearance, and so we think that she was beautiful.

The kinsman, on the other hand, knew Ruth to be a destitute widow from a strange country, who lived only on the gleanings of others' fields. Marrying her might have been a disgrace to his family. He had not paid enough attention to her to learn of her inner beauty, as Boaz had. In the kinsman's eyes, any positive virtues could not possibly outweigh her lowliness of station.

The kinsman turned over his right to the land that had belonged to Elimelech, making it legal for Boaz to purchase it.

> *"Now this was the manner in former time in Israel concerning redeeming and concerning changing, for to confirm all things; a man plucked off his shoe, and gave it to his neighbour: and this was a testimony in Israel.*
>
> *"Therefore the kinsman said unto Boaz, Buy it for thee. So he drew off his shoe.*
>
> *"And Boaz said unto the elders, and unto all the people, Ye are witnesses this day, that I have bought all that was Elimelech's, and all that was Chilion's and Mahlon's, of the hand of Naomi.*
>
> *"Moreover Ruth the Moabitess, the wife of Mahlon, have I purchased to be my wife, to raise up the name of the dead upon his inheritance, that the name of the dead be not cut off from among his brethren, and from the gate of his place: ye are witnesses this day."*—Vss. 7–10.

Instead of a handshake, instead of the signing of an agreement, the kinsman took off his shoe and gave it to Boaz. What does this mean? We can dismiss this as being merely part of the culture of the time, but it actually had a meaning. The shoe was a symbol of declaring ownership of the land by planting the foot on it. The kinsman gave Boaz his shoe, turning his right to claim the land over to Boaz.

When this transaction took place, Boaz turned to the elders who had assembled there: 'You all saw this. You are witnesses that this man has turned over to me the right to redeem Naomi's land.' Boaz, then, was free to purchase the land and marry Ruth.

Let's notice two side-notes here.

1. It appears that Boaz was much older than Ruth. He may have been more nearly the age of Naomi. We know that Naomi was a widow as well. We also know that the land had belonged to Elimelech and was then passed on to Naomi. The question arises, then, Why is this transaction for the purpose of marrying Ruth? Why is it not concerning marrying Naomi?

It seems that this was a choice that Naomi made. When she sent Ruth to the threshing floor the night before, she was turning over to Ruth whatever claim she had to say that Boaz was her kinsman and whatever claim she had to request that he marry her. Naomi did not appear to have the desire to be married; she was trying to secure a husband for Ruth. Remember Ruth 3:1: "Shall I not seek rest for thee, that it may be well with thee?"

Perhaps it was merely because of Naomi's kindness to Ruth. Perhaps Naomi said, "I don't care if I get married again. Let's make sure we find you a husband."

2. It also appears that Boaz could have purchased Naomi's land and married Ruth, and the other kinsman might not have even noticed that a piece of land had slipped through his fingers. It appears that the kinsman knew nothing of any of these matters until Boaz brought

them to his attention. However, Boaz did the honest thing and presented the opportunity to the man who was a nearer kinsman. He made sure he kept everything aboveboard.

What an honorable man Boaz remained in these situations! Many other men would have taken what they wanted without regard to the letter and intent of the law. Instead, Boaz brought the entire matter to the city gate and made the entire transaction with plenty of witnesses.

The more public such a transference of land was made, the less likely there would be any kind of fraud or any kind of later claim by the other party involved. The other kinsman could have later claimed that he had had first right to the land but Boaz had taken it from him. However, in this transaction Boaz made everything public, and the other kinsman turned his right over to Boaz.

Ruth 4:11 goes on, "And all the people that were in the gate, and the elders, said, We are witnesses. The LORD make the woman that is come into thine house like Rachel and like Leah, which two did build the house of Israel: and do thou worthily in Ephratah, and be famous in Beth-lehem." This verse ends in the middle of a sentence, but we will study the next verse in Chapter 11 of this book.

Notice in verse 10 that Boaz said that he had "purchased" Ruth to be his wife. Saying such a thing sounds barbaric to us, but look at it this way. Boaz was a mighty man of wealth. He made the necessary arrangements to be permitted to purchase Naomi's land, and in doing so, he would marry Ruth in the process.

The kinsman with whom Boaz negotiated was very willing to purchase the land, but he did not want to have anything to do with marrying Ruth. He was interested in the land but not in Ruth. Boaz, on the other hand, purchased the land, which was just part of the transaction; but what he was really interested in was Ruth. He saw her inner beauty. He saw that she was virtuous and kind and giving. The land was immaterial.

In Ruth 3:9, Ruth's request was only to "spread . . . thy skirt over thine handmaid; for thou art a near kinsman." There was nothing in her request about land. The land was part of the package, but the treasure was in Ruth. Boaz had land, and he could have purchased more land from another source, but how often does one find such a gem of a wife as he had found in Ruth? We remember that Ruth is the only woman in all the Bible that is called virtuous.

> "Whoso findeth a wife findeth a good thing, and obtaineth favour of the LORD."

> "House and riches are the inheritance of fathers: and a prudent wife is from the LORD."—Prov. 18:22; 19:14.

Houses and riches can come from an inheritance or from hard work. However, a man does not make a good wife; she comes that way. They are few and far between, according to Proverbs 31:10: "Who can find a virtuous woman? for her price is far above rubies." Such a woman is a gift from God.

Lady, make sure your husband can say that his wife is a good thing. Make sure he feels that his wife was a gift to him from God.

Boaz was pleased. He had watched Ruth for long enough to be able to see what a gem she was. God knew how special she was at the outset of the story, but it took some time for everyone else to realize it.

Remember the words of I Samuel 16:7: "The LORD seeth not as man seeth; for man looketh on the outward appearance, but the LORD looketh on the heart."

While it is true that God saw Ruth's heart from the beginning, eventually everyone would know about her strength of character by watching her actions. We need to develop a radiant testimony and then make sure we maintain it.

In chapter 4 of the Book of Ruth, Ruth the Moabitess was reaping the benefits of her virtuous quality. Boaz was pleased to have her; and she was getting a kind, generous man. We say this because of the way we have seen him treat her in the previous chapters.

Ruth's Reward

"So Boaz took Ruth, and she was his wife: and when he went in unto her, the LORD gave her conception, and she bare a son."—Ruth 4:13.

In studying Ruth, we have grown very fond of this lovely young lady who grew up without God. When her Jewish husband died, she stayed with her mother-in-law. She even left all that she had ever known to move to Israel, where the people worshiped the God that she had learned to know through her husband's family.

The people saw excellence of character in Ruth. Boaz asked the Lord to give her a full reward because she had come to trust in Him (Ruth 2:12).

In this chapter, we will see Ruth's reward for her faith and trust in the Lord God of the people of Israel. She had asked Boaz to put her under his protection, which would mean that he would marry her. Boaz was not Naomi's nearest kinsman, so he presented the opportunity to the nearest relative in the presence of witnesses at the gate. That man turned over to Boaz the right to purchase the land, as well as the responsibility to take Ruth.

It appears in the next verses that all those around Ruth and Naomi rejoiced. Apparently there were other people at the gate besides Boaz, the other kinsman and the ten witnesses. This was as one might have imagined. The gate was the place where many people were passing by, and certainly there would have been many who would be very interested in this transaction.

They all asked God's blessing on the union of Boaz and Ruth. Ruth 4:11 says, "And all the people that were in the gate, and the elders, said, We are witnesses. The LORD make the woman that is come into thine house like Rachel and like Leah, which two did build the house of Israel: and do thou worthily in Ephratah, and be famous in Beth-lehem."

When the people pronounced a blessing on Boaz and Ruth, they asked God to make Ruth like Rachel and Leah. Why would they ask God to make her like those two women particularly?

Rachel and Leah (and their handmaidens) are the mothers of those who became the heads of the twelve tribes of Israel. In those days the child who was a result of a union between a man and his wife's handmaiden was named as the child of the man and his wife.

The many, many people in Israel all descended from Jacob, whose name was changed to Israel, and his wives. When they went into Egypt there were already seventy persons; and by the time they left there 430 years later, they were very many in number. Rachel and Leah were fruitful mothers.

The townspeople prayed for Boaz. They prayed that he would do "worthily in Ephratah, and be famous in Beth-lehem." It seems that these two prayers came as a husband-wife package for Boaz and Ruth. Ruth was a virtuous woman. She was good and did right. Boaz was a good, honest man as well as a good, honest businessman. We have mentioned that it was likely that Boaz could have married Ruth and redeemed the land without the notice of the other near kinsman. However, Boaz did the right thing and made the entire transaction public with witnesses at the gate.

The townspeople prayed that Ruth would be a blessing to the family in her home—that is, in their *private* life. They prayed that Boaz would continue to be a blessing to the community—that is, in their *public* life.

They even prayed that Boaz would be "famous" in Bethlehem. It seems strange, does it not, that they would pray for fame for Boaz. According to verse 11, fame is obtained in the life of a person by doing "worthily." A man like Boaz, who knows people at the gate and who is a mighty man of wealth, may develop a reputation for being a good, upstanding man because people learn that they can trust him and depend on him.

On the other hand, such a man may develop a reputation for being a scoundrel if he is dishonest in his dealings and ugly with people. Either way, he will be well known; but if he is good and honest, he will hold a high position in the community and will be held in honor in the opinions of those who know him. That man will be "famous."

The prayer continued in verse 12: "And let thy house be like the house of Pharez, whom Tamar bare unto Judah, of the seed which the LORD shall give thee of this young woman." Why would they pray that their house be like the house of Pharez, the son of Tamar? Who are those people?

Notice first of all that Tamar is one of the four

women mentioned in the genealogy of Christ. In Chapter 5 of this study, we learned that Rahab, the mother of Boaz, is one of these included in that genealogy, and we also know that Ruth is included as well (Matt. 1:5). Both of these women were brought up without a knowledge of God. Both of these women left all that they knew to live with the people of Israel.

Of the four women in Christ's genealogy, Tamar was the first. Matthew 1:3 says, "And Judas begat Phares and Zara of Thamar." Let's look at who she was.

We read about Tamar in Genesis 38. Judah, the fourth-born son of Israel, left his family and found a woman of one of the people of Canaan. Judah acted very unwisely in this case. He left the protective umbrella of his family, found a friend, and then met a woman.

> "And it came to pass at that time, that Judah went down from his brethren, and turned in to a certain Adullamite, whose name was Hirah.
>
> "And Judah saw there a daughter of a certain Canaanite, whose name was Shuah; and he took her, and went in unto her."—Gen. 38:1, 2.

Judah took to himself the daughter of a certain Canaanite, Shuah. They had three children: Er, Onan and Shelah. Shuah's daughter was not the kind of woman Judah should have taken as his own, and we see that the training of the children apparently suffered.

> "And Judah took a wife for Er his firstborn, whose name was Tamar.
>
> "And Er, Judah's firstborn, was wicked in the sight of the LORD; and the LORD slew him.
>
> "And Judah said unto Onan, Go in unto thy

brother's wife, and marry her, and raise up seed to thy brother."—Vss. 6–8.

This was, as we have already seen, a part of the Law of God in Deuteronomy 25:5, 6, that a man marry his brother's wife if he died childless. However, notice that the Law did not come until much later than Genesis 38. Apparently it had already become a custom, or perhaps the Lord had made clear to them that this was to be done. Onan, however, understood that the child born to him and his brother's wife, Tamar, would carry the name of his brother; and he would not accept this duty. If the child would not be named as his, then he would have no child.

> *"And Onan knew that the seed should not be his; and it came to pass, when he went in unto his brother's wife, that he spilled it on the ground, lest that he should give seed to his brother.*
>
> *"And the thing which he did displeased the LORD: wherefore he slew him also.*
>
> *"Then said Judah to Tamar his daughter in law, Remain a widow at thy father's house, till Shelah my son be grown: for he said, Lest peradventure he die also, as his brethren did. And Tamar went and dwelt in her father's house."*—Gen. 38:9–11.

Judah apparently blamed the death of his two boys on Tamar. However, according to the verses we just read, the boys died because of their own wickedness. Judah told Tamar to go home to her own father and remain a widow. Tamar obeyed Judah's instructions; but it seems that Judah never had any intention of allowing Tamar to marry his youngest son, Shelah.

"And in process of time the daughter of Shuah

Judah's wife died; and Judah was comforted, and went up unto his sheepshearers to Timnath, he and his friend Hirah the Adullamite" (vs. 12). Judah's wife died. Then he was going to shear his sheep with his friend Hirah. The time of sheepshearing was apparently a time of much work as well as a time of celebration. It appears that all the sheep were gathered together in an enclosure and were sheared. There was a lot of socializing that went on as well, but it was just the men who were participating. This appears to be the same kind of socializing activity as when the men were harvesting their grain.

> "And it was told Tamar, saying, Behold thy father in law goeth up to Timnath to shear his sheep.
>
> "And she put her widow's garments off from her, and covered her with a vail, and wrapped herself, and sat in an open place, which is by the way to Timnath; for she saw that Shelah was grown, and she was not given unto him to wife."—Vss. 13, 14.

By this time Shelah had grown up, and Judah had not allowed Tamar to be married to him. Did he seriously think that this young lady was the downfall of his sons? Certainly he knew what they were like.

Why, then, did she change her clothes and cover herself with a veil?

Verse 15 goes on, "When Judah saw her, he thought her to be an harlot; because she had covered her face."

Because she covered her face with a veil, he thought she was a harlot. This is in contrast to the attire of harlots in modern times. These days, if a woman is a harlot, her dress will be very skimpy, revealing herself so that men will be enticed by her body. It appears that even the harlots of early Old Testament days had some sense of shame for what they were doing. Because Tamar covered herself with a veil, she was not known.

The story continues: "And he turned unto her by the way, and said, Go to, I pray thee, let me come in unto thee; (for he knew not that she was his daughter in law.) And she said, What wilt thou give me, that thou mayest come in unto me?" (vs. 16).

Notice that Tamar did nothing to entice Judah; she was merely present at an open place. Judah approached her.

> *"And he said, I will send thee a kid from the flock. And she said, Wilt thou give me a pledge, till thou send it?*
>
> *"And he said, What pledge shall I give thee? And she said, Thy signet, and thy bracelets, and thy staff that is in thine hand. And he gave it her, and came in unto her, and she conceived by him."*—Vss. 17, 18.

Judah, thinking that Tamar was a harlot, went in to her. We must question the integrity, the wisdom and the overall character of a man who would go in unto a harlot; but that was what Judah did. She was not a harlot by profession—she was his daughter-in-law; but he did not know that. Judah went in unto this woman, and she conceived, even though he apparently never even saw her face! He never did know who she was.

What a cold, heartless, selfish, fleshly thing that only a horrible man could do! Could God actually use such a man for any good at all? It seems to be the epitome of idiocy for a man to decide to go in to a harlot. There is no possible honorable reason to do so.

It appears interesting that Tamar felt fairly certain that if her father-in-law thought she was a harlot, he would go in unto her. Apparently she knew something of his lowness of character. Yet we know that it was through the lineage of this son of Israel that the Messiah was to come.

We look at this whole affair and say how terrible it is, but the fact is that we are all sinners. God told us that. Judah was wrong. There is no question about it; but God keeps His promises, no matter what. God is gracious and merciful and kind beyond all comprehension. We can be thankful.

God said that the Messiah would come through the line of Judah, and so He did. The promise that the Saviour would come through Judah did not come until the end of Genesis, so that promise was given after this event in the life of Judah.

We must remember that sin is sin, no matter how big or small it is. I am so thankful that God allows sinners to serve Him and that He allows sinners to be used by Him for His work, because I am one of those. In God's eyes, my sin is just as ugly as Judah's sin, even though I spend my life trying to do right. My look of pride or jealousy, which no one may ever detect, is a horrible stench to God. We must never forget that. From our perspective, however, Judah's sin was very grave. He knew better! When God looks at our sin, it is all sin, big or little. It is difficult to imagine, but to God it is all sin.

How would Judah pay her? He promised to give her a kid from his flock. He did not know that she knew him, and she would not trust him to send her something later. So she asked him to give her a pledge. This would be something that he would give to her and would receive back again after she received the kid.

What did Judah give to her? Notice in verse 18, he

asked her to suggest what he should give to her. She wanted his signet, bracelets and staff. He gave them to her.

Why would she request those things? The signet was a ring that was used as a seal; it was a symbol of his authority. It was used to sign documents onto which he would make an impression in wax or some such product. This was Judah's unique seal. The bracelets may have been wide bands that were worn above the elbow. Those items surely had personalized engravings or markings on them as well. In any case, those items would be easily identifiable as his. She was going to be able to use them to convict him later.

While we certainly do not condone Tamar's course of action, let us look at this from her perspective. She had married. In those days, all women wanted to have children, and it was a horrible shame to them if they had none. It was a social disgrace. When her husband died, her father-in-law ordered his next son, Onan, to marry her, thereby perpetuating the name of Er, the deceased brother. Onan wanted no part of having his firstborn child given the name of his brother! He simply refused to have children. God killed him for this act.

Judah wanted Tamar to wait until his youngest son was old enough to marry. It appears that a significant amount of time passed; all the while, Tamar's childbearing days were ticking away. She probably became angry and perhaps even bitter over the whole affair. *I'll show Judah*, she may have thought. ***Judah** will father my child!* Surely we can see this happening in her heart. She took matters into her own hands. After it was over, she simply went home and waited.

"And she arose, and went away, and laid by her

vail from her, and put on the garments of her widow-hood.

"And Judah sent the kid by the hand of his friend the Adullamite, to receive his pledge from the woman's hand: but he found her not.

"Then he asked the men of that place, saying, Where is the harlot, that was openly by the way side? And they said, There was no harlot in this place.

"And he returned to Judah, and said, I cannot find her; and also the men of the place said, that there was no harlot in this place.

"And Judah said, Let her take it to her, lest we be shamed: behold, I sent this kid, and thou hast not found her."—Vss. 19–23.

True to his promise, Judah sent a kid with his friend to give to the harlot. However, there was no harlot. Judah's friend even asked the men of that place where that harlot would be, and they did not know about whom he was talking. They knew of no harlot.

His response in verse 23 is interesting: "Let her take it to her." He was saying, 'Let her have the signet and bracelets and staff.' Then he said, "Lest we be shamed": 'If we keep asking about it, everybody will think I am a fool for trusting such a woman with my things.' The signet was a personal identification, and he was foolish enough to let a harlot take possession of it. It would have been as if he had given her his credit card as a pledge that he would return with payment! People may very well laugh at him for being such a fool.

He was afraid people would laugh at him for trusting the woman with his valuables, but he did not fear God for the sin of adultery that he had committed. What a shame!

"And it came to pass about three months after, that it was told Judah, saying, Tamar thy daughter in law hath played the harlot; and also, behold, she is with child by whoredom. And Judah said, Bring her forth, and let her be burnt" (vs. 24). After learning that Tamar was with child, Judah was outraged and threatened to have her burned. The obvious question to me is, Why was he not asking who the man was who had committed this horrible sin with her? He was not talking about burning him. He was pointing his finger at her.

> *"When she was brought forth, she sent to her father in law, saying, By the man, whose these are, am I with child: and she said, Discern, I pray thee, whose are these, the signet, and bracelets, and staff.*
>
> *"And Judah acknowledged them, and said, She hath been more righteous than I; because that I gave her not to Shelah my son. And he knew her again no more."*—Vss. 25, 26.

He knew immediately that the signet, bracelets and staff were his; he could not deny the markings on them. He could not deny what he had done. He knew immediately that the issue was that he had not given his son to marry her as he had promised. He acknowledged that he was wrong in this matter. The children were his own, but he was never intimate with Tamar again.

> *"And it came to pass in the time of her travail, that, behold, twins were in her womb.*
>
> *"And it came to pass, when she travailed, that the one put out his hand: and the midwife took and bound upon his hand a scarlet thread, saying, This came out first.*
>
> *"And it came to pass, as he drew back his hand,*

*that, behold, his brother came out: and she said,
How hast thou broken forth? this breach be upon
thee: therefore his name was called Pharez.*

*"And afterward came out his brother, that had the
scarlet thread upon his hand: and his name was
called Zarah."*—Vss. 27–30.

Why does it matter which child was born first? The
midwife insisted that Zarah was born first. His hand
came out, and she tied a string around his hand. As the
babies moved around, Pharez actually came out first.
The name *Pharez* means "breaking forth."

In our day, being the firstborn does not really carry
any special name or privilege; but in Old Testament
times, the firstborn became the head of the family at the
father's death. He also received a double portion of the
inheritance; therefore, being the firstborn was a matter
of great significance.

The question of who was firstborn may have been a
matter of contention between Zarah and Pharez. Zarah
may have felt that he should have been the firstborn and
that he had been dealt a wrong not to have received
those privileges.

This was from where Pharez came. So why did the
people in Ruth 4:12 pray that the house of Boaz and
Ruth would be like that of Pharez?

Remember, it is not nearly as important where you
came from as where you are going.

1. We learned that Rahab came from Jericho where
she turned from the idol worship with which she had
grown up, to God. God presents her to us as a great
example of faith in Hebrews 11.

2. We have seen in this book that Ruth turned from the idol worship with which she had grown up, to God. In this very chapter, we are seeing that Ruth was greatly rewarded for her faith in God and obedience to His commands.

What was it about Pharez that made the people want Boaz's house to be like his? It appears that it was only that Pharez was very fruitful: he had many descendents. The people were praying that Boaz and Ruth would be fruitful.

It is also interesting to notice that Pharez and Zarah are both mentioned in Matthew 1:3 in the genealogy. In every other case, only the son who was in the line leading to Christ was mentioned, except for the sons of Judah. Verse 2 says, "Abraham begat Isaac; and Isaac begat Jacob; and Jacob begat Judas and his brethren."

Judah is mentioned because it is through his line that the Lord would be born. His brothers were mentioned because they were the fathers of the tribes of Israel. However, in verse 3, Pharez and Zarah are both mentioned, even though the line of Christ came through Pharez.

> *"So Boaz took Ruth, and she was his wife: and when he went in unto her, the LORD gave her conception, and she bare a son.*
>
> *"And the women said unto Naomi, Blessed be the LORD, which hath not left thee this day without a kinsman, that his name may be famous in Israel.*
>
> *"And he shall be unto thee a restorer of thy life, and a nourisher of thine old age: for thy daughter in law, which loveth thee, which is better to thee than seven sons, hath born him.*

"And Naomi took the child, and laid it in her bosom, and became nurse unto it."—Ruth 4:13–16.

Naomi and Ruth were very thankful for Obed. The townswomen were rejoicing, thanking God for Boaz who took the part of the kinsman in marrying Ruth, carrying on the name of her family.

Naomi had felt that she came back to Israel with nothing, even though she had left with a husband and sons. She had felt that God had worked against her. When she returned she had asked the townspeople to call her Mara, which means "bitter."

"And she said unto them, Call me not Naomi, call me Mara: for the Almighty hath dealt very bitterly with me.

"I went out full, and the LORD hath brought me home again empty: why then call ye me Naomi, seeing the LORD hath testified against me, and the Almighty hath afflicted me?"—1:20, 21.

What a difference when we reach chapter 4! A son is born, and he is called Obed which means "worshiper."

"And the women her neighbours gave it a name, saying, There is a son born to Naomi; and they called his name Obed: he is the father of Jesse, the father of David.

"Now these are the generations of Pharez: Pharez begat Hezron,

"And Hezron begat Ram, and Ram begat Amminadab,

"And Amminadab begat Nahshon, and Nahshon begat Salmon,

"And Salmon begat Boaz, and Boaz begat Obed,

"And Obed begat Jesse, and Jesse begat David."—
Vss. 17–22.

Why is this genealogy included at the end of the Book of Ruth? The lineage is listed from Pharez, the son of Judah, to David. It was from Judah's line that the Saviour was promised. In the genealogy in Matthew, the line is listed from Abraham to David, then from David to Christ. Once again, all the Bible is about Jesus.

Boaz, a Picture of Jesus, Our Redeemer

"Blessed be the LORD, which hath not left thee this day without a kinsman."—Ruth 4:14.

In the beginning of our study of the Book of Ruth, I said these words:

> The Book of Ruth is a little book tucked among the books of history in the Bible. It is a nice story about a girl from "the wrong side of the tracks" who left everything she knew after her husband's death to go to her mother-in-law's homeland, where she found true love and everyone lived happily ever after. We can assuredly say, however, that God gave us this story for a reason much greater than mere entertainment.
>
> There is much truth to be learned from this little book.

Indeed, we have learned many things. God's grace and mercy continue to shine forth from the words of this little Book of Ruth. Boaz took Ruth as his wife even though she was a Moabitess. He saw in her a desire to know the Lord.

In I Corinthians 10 Paul reminded the Corinthian believers of some of the Old Testament accounts when the people of Israel did not trust or obey God. He was warning them to learn from the mistakes of those who had not responded to the Lord as they should. The Old

Testament accounts had a purpose greater than merely to tell us what happened to those people.

Paul wrote, "Now all these things happened unto them for ensamples: and they are written for our admonition, upon whom the ends of the world are come" (I Cor. 10:11). That means that the events of the Old Testament are there to teach us something. The events of the Old Testament were real and about real people. They lived just like you and I live. They had emotions just like you and I have emotions. They experienced fear, frustration, pain, love, and joy just like you and I do.

God has given the events of the Old Testament to be "ensamples" for us. Some Bibles may simply change the word "ensamples" to "examples," but it is not the same word. The word "ensample" means "to strike with a die," which would make an imprint. The Old Testament accounts are supposed to make an impression on us.

God gave them to us for a reason. Some will teach us what to do. Some will teach us what not to do. Some will encourage us. Some will show us God's awesome power. Some will show us God's great mercy which is extended to us continually even though we continue to sin. We also learn about the wrath of God in the face of continued willful disobedience. There are many lessons to be learned from the Old Testament.

The entire Bible is about God's work in the lives of people. It is about the redemption of mankind. In Ruth we find a wonderful picture of Jesus in the character of Boaz. Boaz was the kinsman who redeemed the land for Naomi and redeemed Ruth from the destitution of her widowhood. Jesus is our Saviour who redeemed us from our sin. We have no hope of escaping the fires of Hell without His redeeming grace.

In Ruth 2:12 Boaz prayed that the Lord would "recompense thy work, and a full reward be given thee of the LORD God of Israel, under whose wings thou art come to trust." This gives us a picture of a large bird tenderly protecting her young under her strong wings. Ruth came to trust the Lord and rest under His protective power. In Ruth 3:9 Ruth asked Boaz to spread his "skirt" over her because he was a near kinsman. The word that is translated "wings" in Ruth 2:12 is the same as the word that is translated "skirt" in Ruth 3:9.

We read the same English word in Matthew 23:37. Jesus laments over Jerusalem who killed the prophets whom God sent to give them instructions from Him. He said, "How often would I have gathered thy children together, even as a hen gathereth her chickens under her wings, and ye would not!"

God offered His protective covering for the people of Israel, but they would not listen. The Gentile people, on the other hand, received His Word gladly and were saved. They received His offer of redemption gladly, even though the Jews had rejected it.

I. Qualifications of a Redeemer

How could a man be a redeemer for someone else? What qualifications did he have to meet in order to act as a redeemer, as Boaz did for Ruth?

1. He had to have the *right* to redeem. The redeemer must be a near kinsman.

"If thy brother be waxen poor, and hath sold away

some of his possession, and if any of his kin come to redeem it, then shall he redeem that which his brother sold."

"And if a sojourner or stranger wax rich by thee, and thy brother that dwelleth by him wax poor, and sell himself unto the stranger or sojourner by thee, or to the stock of the stranger's family:

"After that he is sold he may be redeemed again; one of his brethren may redeem him:

"Either his uncle, or his uncle's son, may redeem him, or any that is nigh of kin unto him of his family may redeem him; or if he be able, he may redeem himself."—Lev. 25:25, 47–49.

If a man is poor and sells his land, a kinsman may redeem the land, or buy it back. A kinsman may pay the price for redemption.

If a man is poor and sells himself to be a slave, a kinsman may redeem him, or buy him back. A kinsman may pay the price for redemption.

Boaz was a near kinsman and had the right, as the near relative, to redeem the land (buy it back) and to redeem Ruth (to marry her and raise up seed for Mahlon).

2. He had to have the *power* to redeem. The redeemer must have the resources necessary to pay the price for redemption.

Even if a man is a near kinsman, if he does not have enough money to purchase the land, he cannot redeem it. If he does not have enough money to purchase his brother who has been a slave, he cannot redeem him. Boaz was Ruth's redeemer, and he was Naomi's redeemer with regard to the purchase of her land. He was, as we learned in Ruth 2:1, a kinsman and a mighty man of wealth.

3. He had to have the *will* to redeem. If the kinsman had no desire to effect the redemption that was needed, no redemption would take place.

> *"And Er, Judah's firstborn, was wicked in the sight of the* LORD; *and the* LORD *slew him.*
>
> *"And Judah said unto Onan, Go in unto thy brother's wife, and marry her, and raise up seed to thy brother.*
>
> *"And Onan knew that the seed should not be his; and it came to pass, when he went in unto his brother's wife, that he spilled it on the ground, lest that he should give seed to his brother."*—Gen. 38:7–9.

Apparently Onan was capable of producing children; but he was not willing to redeem Tamar, his sister-in-law, in the matter of raising up seed for his brother. God was not pleased with this action, and He killed Onan; however, Tamar was not redeemed from her childless state.

Boaz had the right, the power and the will to redeem Ruth from her state of widowhood and to redeem Naomi's land.

Boaz was not the nearest kinsman, but he promised he would talk with the closest kinsman and that either he or the other kinsman would do the part of the kinsman redeemer. At no time did Boaz treat Ruth as being any less than he himself was. In fact, he blessed her (Ruth 2:12). He encouraged and helped her. When she asked him to spread his skirt over her (3:9), he promised her that he would provide a home for her: "Tarry this night, and it shall be in the morning, that if he will perform unto thee the part of a kinsman, well; let him do the kinsman's part: but if he will not do the part of a kinsman to thee, then will I do the part of a kinsman to thee" (vs. 13).

II. A Beautiful Picture of Jesus, Our Redeemer

We are all sinners. We are trapped in the slavery of sin. We cannot avoid it, and we cannot deny it. We were born that way. Your beautiful baby that you think is so very precious and sweet is a sinner. He got it from you! Your husband, your parents, your children, your pastor, and all the ladies reading this book are sinners!

> *"The fool hath said in his heart, There is no God. They are corrupt, they have done abominable works, there is none that doeth good."*
>
> *"They are all gone aside, they are all together become filthy: there is none that doeth good* [and just in case anyone objects, the Lord insists], *no, not one."*—Ps. 14:1, 3.
>
> *"As it is written, There is none righteous* [and just in case anyone objects, the Lord insists], *no, not one:*
>
> *"There is none that understandeth, there is none that seeketh after God.*
>
> *"They are all gone out of the way, they are together become unprofitable; there is none that doeth good* [and just in case anyone objects, the Lord insists], *no, not one."*
>
> *"For all have sinned, and come short of the glory of God."*
>
> *"For the wages of sin is death."*—Rom. 3:10–12, 23; 6:23.

We are all in need of a Kinsman Redeemer. If a man

sold himself to be a slave, he needed a kinsman who would redeem him (Lev. 25:48). We are slaves of sin, and the price that is required to pay for our sin is death. We have no hope in our own merit.

1. Christ has the *right* to redeem us.

God promised the people of Israel that He would send a Prophet. He would come from the people of Israel. He would be one of them.

> "The LORD thy God will raise up unto thee a Prophet from the midst of thee, of thy brethren, like unto me; unto him ye shall hearken."
>
> "I will raise them up a Prophet from among their brethren, like unto thee, and will put my words in his mouth; and he shall speak unto them all that I shall command him.
>
> "And it shall come to pass, that whosoever will not hearken unto my words which he shall speak in my name, I will require it of him."—Deut. 18:15, 18, 19.

That Prophet was the promised Messiah, Jesus. Notice that the Lord tells Moses that the Prophet would be "of thy brethren" (vs. 15); speaking to Moses, God says the Prophet would be "like unto thee" (vs. 18).

Paul wrote, "Concerning his Son Jesus Christ our Lord, which was made of the seed of David according to the flesh" (Rom. 1:3). Jesus was made of the seed of David. He was a kinsman. He was a Jew. He was part of the family. He has the right to redeem us.

2. Christ has the *power* to redeem us.

The Lord said that the promised Prophet would be "like unto me" (Deut. 18:15). He would be like God Himself. John 10:30 says, "I and my Father are one."

A short time before Jesus went to the cross, He prayed, "Holy Father, keep through thine own name those whom thou hast given me, that they may be one, as we are" (17:11).

> "In the beginning was the Word, and the Word was with God, and the Word was God.
>
> "The same was in the beginning with God.
>
> "All things were made by him; and without him was not any thing made that was made.
>
> "In him was life; and the life was the light of men."
>
> "And the Word was made flesh, and dwelt among us, (and we beheld his glory, the glory as of the only begotten of the Father,) full of grace and truth."— 1:1–4, 14.

The Word of God in John 1:1 was Jesus. Jesus was God. Jesus *is* God. As God, Jesus has the power to redeem us. He has the necessary resources to redeem us. We often say that He took our punishment for us. That is not really accurate, although it makes perfect sense to us. Romans 6:23 says, "The wages of sin is death." Death is what we owe for our sin; it is our debt. Jesus paid our debt; He paid what we owed for our sin.

Jesus had the resources to pay the price for my sin. He is God, and He had no sin. He paid the price, and then He rose again. The price was paid; therefore, He did not have to stay dead.

The resurrection proved that our sins were paid. If I offered to pay your sin debt for you, it would mean nothing. I do not have the necessary resources. I have sin of my own for which I owe a debt. If I died in payment for sins, it would be my own sins for which I was dying.

Your debt of sins would still be unpaid. When you died, you would pay your own debt. However, you and I would never rise again because our debt would never be paid. We would suffer for eternity in Hell with no hope of ever making the final payment for our sins.

Jesus, however, had the power, the resources, to be our Redeemer.

3. Christ was *willing* to redeem us.

Even though Jesus has the power to redeem us, if He had not been willing, we would still be dead in our sins; but Jesus was willing to go to the cross for us.

> *"I am the good shepherd: the good shepherd giveth his life for the sheep."*

> *"As the Father knoweth me, even so know I the Father: and I lay down my life for the sheep."*—
> John 10:11, 15.

Jesus is the Good Shepherd. The Good Shepherd loves His sheep more than His own life. Since the wages of sin is death, Jesus was willing to pay that price.

Why was Jesus willing to do such a thing for us? He and the Father did not want us to have to pay the awful price for our sin—suffer in Hell for eternity. He loves us. He is sitting at the right hand of the Father, making a place for us where we can be with Him forever and ever.

> *"The Lord is…not willing that any should perish, but that all should come to repentance."*—II Pet. 3:9.

> *"For the Son of Man is come to seek and to save that which was lost."*—Luke 19:10.

> *"Let not your heart be troubled: ye believe in God,*

believe also in me.

"In my Father's house are many mansions: if it were not so, I would have told you. I go to prepare a place for you.

"And if I go and prepare a place for you, I will come again, and receive you unto myself; that where I am, there ye may be also."—John 14:1–3.

What a wonderful heavenly Father we have! What a wonderful Saviour, Jesus, we have!

There is one question that begs to be answered from this story of Ruth, however. In light of the picture of Jesus in these pages, what about the other kinsman? What does he represent?

The other kinsman is a picture of the law. Notice that he said twice in Ruth 4:6, "I cannot redeem it." What did this mean? Notice that he did not say that he did not have the

1. *right* to redeem it. He was a nearer kinsman than Boaz. He had the right.

2. *power* to redeem it. It appears that he had land and funds. He had the resources.

3. *willingness* to redeem it. He had already said that he would redeem the land.

Those were not the problems. No, the problem was that he *couldn't.* The other kinsman, our picture of the law in the Book of Ruth, could not redeem.

Many people in the Old Testament thought that they could obtain redemption by keeping the law. Hebrews 10:1–3 says,

"For the law having a shadow of good things to

come, and not the very image of the things, can never with those sacrifices which they offered year by year continually make the comers thereunto perfect.

"For then would they not have ceased to be offered? because that the worshippers once purged should have had no more conscience of sins.

"But in those sacrifices there is a remembrance again made of sins every year."

The law was not designed to redeem us. The law was given to us to show us that we need a Redeemer. The law was given to us to remind us over and over again of how sinful we are. If the sacrifices had been able to purge away sins, the sins would have been purged, and the Old Testament saints would have been able to stop offering the sacrifices.

There is no reward for keeping the law. No one has ever been stopped by a policeman who has commended him for stopping at the stop sign and obeying the speed limits and the traffic lights. No, you are not rewarded for keeping the law, but you are fined or imprisoned for breaking the law. Galatians 3:11 says, "But that no man is justified by the law in the sight of God, it is evident: for, The just shall live by faith."

The other kinsman could not redeem Ruth. He is a picture of the law.

What about Ruth? Is she part of the picture at all? Isn't this book about her?

Oh, yes! This is so exciting! Just as Boaz is a picture of Jesus, our Redeemer, Ruth is a picture of the Gentile bride of Christ! That is who most of us are! She was not a Jew. She was not a part of the family of the chosen people of God. She was an alien, a foreigner, an outsider; but when she came to know the Lord, she gave up all that she had known and all that she had and followed God.

The blessings that God offered were available to Ruth. No, she did not grow up in the "right" kind of family; she did not go to the "right" kind of church; but she believed, trusted, wanted, and followed God. She married Boaz and became a part of the family, even became a part of the lineage of Christ.

So it is with us. Many of us are Gentiles. We are not a part of the chosen people of God. However, if we understand that we are sinners and therefore have no right to the things of God (Rom. 3:23), and if we accept the payment Christ made for our sins when He died on the cross, we can have a home in Heaven with Him forever and ever. It is a gift (6:23).

He showed us that He loved us when He died on the cross (5:8). He told us that He wants us to live with Him forever and that He will come again and get us so that we can be with Him (John 14:2, 3). All we have to do is ask Him for the gift of eternal life that He offers (Rom. 10:13).

Ruth is a beautiful picture of the bride of Christ, and that is who we are! She never acted as though Boaz owed her anything. She went to his fields, expecting nothing and being thankful for everything.

We can learn from Ruth that God owes us nothing but provides everything. He is far greater than we are; but He loves, accepts and encourages us and provides a home for us. He never treats us as though He has no time or energy for us. We can rest, as Ruth did in chapter 3, knowing that He can take care of every situation that comes our way.

God is great. God is good. We ought to be thankful for everything He gives to us. We ought to accept His gracious gift of eternal life that we cannot earn or buy.

Boaz, in the Book of Ruth, is a picture of Christ, our Redeemer.

Save Your Life or Lose It?

"For whosoever will save his life shall lose it: but whosoever will lose his life for my sake, the same shall save it."—Luke 9:24.

In this little Book of Ruth, we have looked at a number of people. Some received great blessings from God, while others experienced devastating losses. In this chapter, we are going to conclude our study of Ruth by looking at the results that people experienced depending on how they responded to God. Some of these will be obvious because we have already discussed them in this study, while others will be examples that have been taken from other parts of Scripture.

The Lord will bless us beyond anything we can imagine if we will simply trust and obey Him. We must settle this in our hearts: Trusting and obeying God bring- blessings.

The opposite is also true: Lack of trust in God and lack of obedience to Him make us ineligible for great blessings from Him. We are often very busy making sure we have the necessities of life. Sometimes we will even compromise on the clear commands of God in order to realize financial gain. How dangerous it is to ignore God's commands and walk away from Him, thinking that it will make our lives more prosperous.

Proverbs 3:5–7 says,

> "Trust in the LORD with all thine heart; and lean not unto thine own understanding.
>
> "In all thy ways acknowledge him, and he shall direct thy paths.
>
> "Be not wise in thine own eyes: fear the LORD, and depart from evil."

Sometimes the choices in life are made very clear. When the Christian realizes he simply needs to depart from evil, it greatly narrows his options.

> "O taste and see that the LORD is good: blessed is the man that trusteth in him.
>
> "O fear the LORD, ye his saints: for there is no want to them that fear him.
>
> "The young lions do lack, and suffer hunger: but they that seek the LORD shall not want any good thing."—Ps. 34:8–10.

> "Behold, I set before you this day a blessing and a curse;
>
> "A blessing, if ye obey the commandments of the LORD your God, which I command you this day:
>
> "And a curse, if ye will not obey the commandments of the LORD your God."—Deut. 11:26–28.

The Lord is clear. If you obey Him, follow His commandments and stay away from anything that will get your heart and mind off Him, He will bless you.

I. Ruth

We saw in Chapter 3 of our study that Ruth left her home, her family and friends as well as the worship of the false god, Chemosh. She traveled with her mother-in-law, Naomi, to the land of Israel. They were both widows and had no means of support. Perhaps they thought they would surely spend the rest of their lives together, having nothing to their name; but Ruth went with Naomi because she wanted to follow God. Orpah had returned to Moab to follow her gods, but Ruth refused to be persuaded to stay in her homeland.

> *"And she* [Naomi] *said, Behold, thy sister in law is gone back unto her people, and unto her gods: return thou after thy sister in law.*
>
> *"And Ruth said, Intreat me not to leave thee, or to return from following after thee: for whither thou goest, I will go; and where thou lodgest, I will lodge: thy people shall be my people, and thy God my God."*—Ruth 1:15,16.

Ruth left everything she knew to follow God. Perhaps she assumed that she would have nothing. She did not presume upon anyone to give her anything. She got up in the morning and went to find a field in which someone would allow her to glean. She assumed that she would have to live from day to day doing the best she could to sustain herself and her mother-in-law.

However, by the end of the Book of Ruth, she has been provided for, she is married to a man who is a mighty man of wealth, and she has a child. She is no longer gleaning in the fields just to survive from day to day. She is married to the wealthy landowner! She was not gleaning in the fields; she owned the fields!

Boaz told Ruth that everyone knew she was a virtuous woman, so we can be sure that God knew it too. Ruth had left all she had to follow God.

II. Naomi and Elimelech

On the other hand, Naomi and Elimelech already lived in the land of Israel—the land that God promised to the Jews. When a famine came in the land of Israel, they decided that they would go to the land of Moab, where apparently there was food. They had two sons who would be growing up with people who did not know the Lord. They thought that the move to Moab would enhance their situation, but they were moving away from God.

Their situation did not improve. Elimelech died in the land of Moab. Naomi became a single mother of two sons. The two boys married girls from Moab, and then the two boys died also. Only Naomi and her two daughters-in-law were left.

Instead of realizing an improvement in their situation because of the move to Moab, they lost all. They had left the land given to the Jews and moved in with the world.

III. Rahab

We learned about Rahab, Boaz's mother, in Chapter 5. She was willing to betray her own people and save the spies who had gone into Jericho from the nation of Israel. She thought that God was so powerful that He would surely defeat the city of Jericho even though its citizens had felt completely safe prior to the arrival of the Israelites.

Rahab left everything she knew so that she could be on God's side. God thought that she was a fine example of one who trusted Him. She is even included in the Hall of Fame of the Faithful in Hebrews 11:31. God presents her in Scripture as one who is an example to others.

There are numerous examples in Scripture of those who obeyed God and were blessed by Him, as well as examples of those who walked away from God in an effort to improve their circumstances. We can see just by looking at the stories of those people that it is always wise to obey and follow God but never wise to turn away from Him.

IV. Abram

God called Abram when he was living in Ur of the Chaldees (Gen. 12:1–3). God told him to leave his homeland, his family and all that he knew. He did not tell Abram where to go. He said He would show him where He wanted him when he arrived at that place. Abram obeyed. He left his home.

The Lord greatly blessed Abram materially. He was so wealthy with flocks and herds that he and his nephew, Lot, could not live together anymore. There simply was not enough water and pasture for all the animals if they stayed together. When they decided to part ways, Abram allowed Lot to choose which direction he would travel. Abram would go the other way. He trusted God when Lot chose the good land. God had blessed him, and he would continue to trust God to bless him. Whichever direction he went, he would be certain to remain under the protective hand of God.

V. Lot

As long as Lot stayed with Abram, he continued to be wealthy as well. When Abram allowed Lot to choose first which way he would go, he looked at the pasture and the growth of the crops (Gen. 13:10–13). The fact that the beautiful land was near the wicked city of that the beautiful land was near the wicked city of Sodom did not deter him from moving there. When the city of Sodom was overthrown by the mighty hand of God, Lot lost everything.

Lot moved toward the world in an effort to sustain his wealth, and he lost everything.

This truth can be seen all through the Bible, even from the very beginning.

VI. Adam and Eve

In the beginning, God created all things beautiful. The first man and woman lived in the beautiful Garden of Eden. They had no fear of the animals, they had all that they could eat, and they had face-to-face fellowship with God. It was a perfect environment. They could do anything they wanted to do, except that they were not permitted to eat fruit from the tree in the middle of the Garden.

They had everything, but Eve allowed the serpent to convince her that she would be wiser if she ate the fruit from the tree in the middle of the Garden (Gen. 3:1–7). After she ate the fruit, she gave some to Adam, and he ate also. They took what they thought they wanted, but they lost all the wonderful blessings of God, and they lost the face-to-face fellowship with Him.

In the Garden, all the fruit grew beautifully. They went out of the Garden where they had weeds and this-tles and had to work hard by the sweat of their brows to make things grow just so they could eat. They could have lived forever in the Garden of Eden—a paradise; but they had a hard life outside the Garden, and then they had to die.

through death at the hand of Cain, his brother. They lost Cain to the world. Genesis 4:16 says, "And Cain went out from the presence of the LORD." They disobeyed God in an effort to have something they thought they wanted, but they lost many blessings.

VII. Noah

In Genesis 6 we learn that man had become so wicked that God would send a great Flood to kill everything and everyone. However, verse 8 says, "But Noah found grace in the eyes of the LORD."

In the middle of rampant wickedness all around him, Noah remained good and right in the sight of the Lord. He was a "preacher of righteousness" (II Pet. 2:5). God gave him instructions to build the ark. Noah "became heir of the righteousness which is by faith" (Heb. 11:7). Noah trusted God even though he was the only one doing so.

VIII. Moses

When Moses was born, the Egyptians were trying to rid the Hebrew nation of its boy babies. Moses' parents hid him for as long as they could. Then they made a little boat to float him in the river where Pharaoh's daughter would find him.

He grew up in the palace as the son of Pharaoh's daughter. He was being groomed to be the next pharaoh. He had all the privileges and opportunities that the world could offer him.

However, "it came to pass in those days, when Moses was grown, that he went out unto his brethren, and looked on their burdens" (Exod. 2:11).

"By faith Moses, when he was come to years, refused to be called the son of Pharaoh's daughter;

"Choosing rather to suffer affliction with the people of God, than to enjoy the pleasures of sin for a season;

"Esteeming the reproach of Christ greater riches than the treasures in Egypt."—Heb. 11:24–26.

It seemed that Moses was giving up all that had been provided for him by the wealth of the Pharaoh of Egypt. It seemed that Moses had nothing for the rest of his life. He led a stubborn nation of people through a wilderness where there were no comforts of any kind. However, Moses had God.

Proverbs 22:1 says, "A good name is rather to be chosen than great riches." Moses left the world to follow God and is known by all, even to this day, as a great man of God.

IX. David

David was anointed by Samuel to be the next king of Israel when he was but a young person. However, he had to wait until the time was right for him to be the next king. As David grew, Saul learned of his soundness of character and saw that the people loved him. Saul became jealous and began to hunt David down to kill him.

On one occasion, David was hiding in a cave when Saul and his men came looking for him. Saul went into the very cave where David and his men were hiding. David's men wanted him to kill Saul. David refused, saying, "I will not put forth mine hand against my lord; for he is the LORD's anointed" (I Sam. 24:10). He was the king, and David refused to kill him. David determined that he would continue to do right despite danger. He allowed the Lord to determine when Saul's end would be.

God called David "a man after his own heart" (I Sam. 13:14). David was not perfect his entire life, but God saw his heart. He loved the Lord and responded to God's leading in a way that pleased God. Eventually Saul died in battle, and then David became king. David had done right, and God was pleased.

X. Daniel

Daniel had been captured and carried away to Babylon. He determined to obey and trust God even in that heathen land. The king was very impressed with Daniel, and he was eventually elevated to a very high position in the kingdom.

In Daniel 6, the other presidents in that kingdom were jealous. Why had this man been promoted to such a high honor? He was not even Babylonian! They decided to try to dig up some "dirt" on Daniel so that they could discredit him and get rid of him. There was no "dirt" on Daniel. He had lived a life faithful to God.

They made a new law all because of Daniel. It was against the law to pray to anyone but Darius. They had Daniel right where they wanted him. If he didn't pray, he would be showing that he did not really trust God. Then they would know that he was not all that he claimed to be. If he prayed, they could have him thrown into the lions' den, and he would be dead, or so they thought.

What would Daniel do? He stood. He continued to pray. Then when he was thrown into the lions' den, he had nothing but his faith in God. The Lord stopped the mouths of the lions. Daniel was saved, and God was glorified. Daniel had remained faithful to God through everything. He is known to us today as a great man of God.

Let us remember that Daniel was in Babylon because he had been carried away out of Jerusalem, which God had allowed to happen because the nation of Israel had disobeyed God. The people had been worshiping false gods and turning their backs on the one true God of the universe. However, Daniel had remained faithful.

Just as Noah was a shining example of a man who stayed true to God when all around him were turning their backs on God, so Daniel had remained faithful to God when those around him had turned their backs on God. In that heathen land, the Babylonians would not have known or cared if he was following God's commands.

Daniel is known to us today as a great man of God. God was pleased with him.

XI. The Twelve Apostles

Surely we cannot end this little exercise without looking at the twelve men whom Jesus called to be His closest disciples. They left their businesses and homes to follow a Man who spoke with power like no other had spoken. Jesus had followers, but there were others who thought He was a lunatic. Among those who thought that were the religious leaders whom the people had learned to revere. It was a "big deal" for the apostles to follow Jesus. In so doing, they were violating the teachings of the religious leaders.

"And Jesus, walking by the sea of Galilee, saw two brethren, Simon called Peter, and Andrew his brother, casting a net into the sea: for they were fishers.

"And he saith unto them, Follow me, and I will make you fishers of men.

"And they straightway left their nets, and followed him."—Matt. 4:18–20.

They simply picked up and left. The story goes on.

"And going on from thence, he saw other two brethren, James the son of Zebedee, and John his brother, in a ship with Zebedee their father, mending their nets; and he called them.

"And they immediately left the ship and their father, and followed him."—Vss. 21, 22

They simply picked up and left. In Luke 5, Simon Peter had been fishing all night but was catching nothing. Jesus told him to go out into the deep and drop his net again. When Peter obeyed, there were so many fish that the ships began to sink. Peter was amazed. Jesus called Peter to follow Him.

"And when they had brought their ships to land, they forsook all, and followed him."

"And after these things he [Jesus] went forth, and saw a publican, named Levi, sitting at the receipt of custom: and he said unto him, Follow me.

"And he left all, rose up, and followed him."— Luke 5:11, 27, 28.

He simply picked up and left. Each one, individually, was willing to leave what he had and what he knew, to follow Jesus.

XII. Paul

Saul of Tarsus was a Pharisee. As a young man, he was being groomed to hold a high position in the ranks of the Pharisees. He could have had notoriety among the people. He probably would have had all that he wanted from a material standpoint. He determined to use his time and energy ridding the world of those who claimed the name of Jesus. This mission was certainly very popular among the ranks of the Jewish leaders.

However, God saved Saul's soul, and he became the apostle Paul. His life changed completely. Initially, the Christians would not listen to him because they did not trust him. Had he really given his life to the Lord, or was he merely trying to gain a following in order to gather all the Christians together so that he could capture and imprison them?

At the same time, the Jewish leaders would not listen to him because he had betrayed his position. He was not one of them anymore.

Paul's life became difficult. While he had followers in some places, he met with opposition in many areas.

"...in labours more abundant, in stripes above measure, in prisons more frequent, in deaths oft.

"Of the Jews five times received I forty stripes save one.

"Thrice was I beaten with rods, once was I stoned, thrice I suffered shipwreck, a night and a day I have been in the deep;

"In journeyings often, in perils of waters, in perils of robbers, in perils by mine own countrymen, in perils by the heathen, in perils in the city, in perils in the wilderness, in perils in the sea, in perils among false brethren;

"In weariness and painfulness, in watchings often, in hunger and thirst, in fastings often, in cold and nakedness."—II Cor. 11:23–27.

He had a rough time, but Paul was thankful that God had called him and that he had obeyed the Lord throughout his life. We see his thankful spirit in Philippians 3:8, 9:

"Yea doubtless, and I count all things but loss for the excellency of the knowledge of Christ Jesus my Lord: for whom I have suffered the loss of all things, and do count them but dung [I lost all those things, but it just does not matter], *that I may win Christ,*

"And be found in him, not having mine own righteousness, which is of the law, but that which is through the faith of Christ, the righteousness which is of God by faith."

The things that had been so important to him became meaningless in light of possessing the righteousness of God through Christ.

When his life was over, only what he had done for the Lord was important.

"For I am now ready to be offered, and the time of my departure is at hand.

"I have fought a good fight, I have finished my course, I have kept the faith:

"Henceforth there is laid up for me a crown of righteousness, which the Lord, the righteous judge, shall give me at that day: and not to me only, but unto all them also that love his appearing."—II Tim. 4:6–8.

When your life is over, the most important things you will have done will be what you did for the Lord. Paul's life did become very difficult, but he wrote a large portion of the New Testament that we hold in our hands today. He obeyed God. The blessings he received may not have been material blessings, but they were blessings of a greater sort.

Surely we could cite many more examples from Scripture to show us this truth: If you follow God, He will lead you and bless you; but if you turn away from God, His hand of blessing will be lifted from you. How sad that would be!

Follow God, no matter what.

Bibliography

Henry, Matthew. *Matthew Henry's Commentary on the Whole Bible.* Mclean, Virginia: MacDonald Publishing Company.

Hester, H. Richard. *Old Testament Bible History,* Blacktown, NSW, Australia.

Hubbard, Jr., Roberts L. *The Go'el in Ancient Israel: Theological Reflections on an Israelite Institution,* Denver Conservative Baptist Seminary

Josephus, Flavius. *The Complete Works of Josephus,* Kregel Publications, Grand Rapids, Michigan

The King James Study Bible for Women, Thomas Nelson Publishers, Nashville, Tennessee.

Knox, James W. *HolyWomen: a Study Guide for Christian Ladies,* Deland, Florida.

Packer, J.I. and M.C. Tenney, Editors. *Illustrated Manners and Customs of the Bible,* Thomas Nelson Publishers, Nashville, Tennessee.

Spurgeon, Charles H. *Sermons on Women of the Bible,* Hendrickson Publishers, Peabody, Massachusetts.

Zorn, Walter D. *Ancient City Gates,* Lincoln Christian College, Lincoln, Illinois.

For a complete list of available
books, please go to
swordofthelord.com.